From the editor

It was during a committee meeting that Don Foster, Chairman of the 'Friends', asked for suggestions to raise funds for the Theatre which would also mark the three Anniversaries we have this year - (The Good Old Days began 60 years ago, The 'Friends' of the Theatre, started by Peter Sandeman, is 25 years old and it is 25 years since Leeds City Council bought the Theatre) - when I came up with the idea of a 'Book of Memories' in celebration of these special Anniversaries but also, in part, because my dear friend Norman Collier wanted to tell me what the City Varieties meant to him. Each time we met he started the conversation but always got waylaid - (That was Norman, he usually went into some routine or other!) - and passed away before having the chance to express his thoughts.

I wondered how many more fellow artistes would like the chance to say what they thought about this extraordinary theatre which means so much to so many people. I decided there and then to get as many artistes as possible to recount a few words about their time there.

This is the result and I thank each and every artiste who took the time and trouble to reply to my pleas for their involvement. Immense thanks too must go to all the advertisers who made it possible to produce this collection. Thank you too to the general public who have added another aspect. All lovely stories, now on record forever.

I hope you enjoy reading them as much as I have.

Caroline

I would like to thank everyone who has helped in the creation of this collection, and particularly Peter White (The British Music Hall Society), Jo Blake (The Max Miller Appreciation Society), Valerie Mann (Equity), Pam and Colin Ford (Derby & Nottingham Music Hall Association), who are computer wizards, Denise and Richard Shillitoe for proof reading and removing the too numerous 'coma's', Rose Gibson (Leeds Library & Information Services), Sylvia Thompson, for her interest and generous donation and my long suffering husband John, who has kept everything going whilst I've been sat at the computer for months.

I'm also hugely grateful to Tom, Charles and Mark at Technoprint, who looked after the design, artwork and print production with such skill and care.

But mainly thanks to all the advertisers without whom this book could not have been published, to you the reader for buying it and to all those wonderful artistes and members of the public who wanted to help me achieve an everlasting tribute to the World Famous Leeds City Varieties Music Hall and to celebrate our three anniversaries this year.

Typeset and Printed by Technoprint Group, Morley, Leeds
Published by Caroline Fields. First Edition, October 2013.

To Caroline
Congratulations!
Happiness
Ken Dodd

I am so pleased to be part of this wonderful

Book of Memories

which will be enjoyed by future generations

celebrating

60 years of The Good Old Days
25 years of 'The Friends' and
25 years of Leeds City Council safeguarding.

I shall always treasure happy memories of playing the
City Varieties Music Hall.

My very first television appearance
there was on 11th March, 1955
and I have had the privilege of having
Many Happy Returns to the City Varieties stage.

The audiences are wonderful,
The Staff and 'Friends' fabulous and
I just love this place so much.

Long may it continue to be a true Variety Theatre.
Kindest regards to Everyone:-
The Audiences, The Artistes, The Crew, The Staff
And 'The Friends' of this Wonderful Theatre.

Ken Dodd OBE

Knotty Ash

BARNEY COLEHAN MBE

1914 - 1991

Major Barney Colehan MBE (Christened Bernard), was born in Calverley, Pudsey, Leeds on the 19th January 1914. His longest running success was *The Good Old Days*, which began in 1953, was on air for thirty years and ended in 1983. He was honoured by Her Majesty The Queen in the New Years honours list in 1981 for his services to the Entertainment Industry.

From humble beginnings - his father worked in a nearby mill and his mother white-stoned the steps for the neighbours to bring in more money - Barney, who in later life was fondly called, 'The Moustachioed Maestro', grew up in the Aireborough suburbs which were renowned for amateur theatre.

He became involved in amateur theatrical companies and as well as acting in several productions, began directing and later became President of Guiseley Amateur Operatic Society.

During the war, Barney served in the Army as a Major and became attached to the BFBS (The British Forces Broadcasting Service). This was a radio service set up by the British War Office in 1943 to entertain and inform British troops overseas.

When the war ended, he was hand-picked to work for the BBC where his first success as a producer was *Have A Go* - a radio game show with English actor and radio presenter, Wilfred Pickles OBE (1904-1978), which ran from 1946 to 1967. When the contestants won Wilfred would shout, "Give 'em the money, Barney". This series attracted over 20 million listeners and would regularly produce a mailbag of 5,000 letters. Contestants could earn £1/19/11d.

In 1963, Barney had the idea of making a TV version of the popular Radio Luxembourg show *Teen and Twenty Disc Club*. This would later become *Top of the Pops*. In 1966, Barney brought *It's a Knockout* to our TV screens. He oversaw the first ten series, which ran for over 16 years.

Barney worked with Cecil Harry Korer, a television producer and executive who worked on *Top Of The Pops* from its first show in 1964. Cecil also commissioned *Countdown*. (It's rumoured that the computer on *Countdown* is named after Cecil - Countdown Electronic Computer In Leeds.) Barney and Cecil got on well and when Barney revived *The Good Old Days* for The BBC, Cecil was alongside.

Barney's unique idea was to re-create a Music Hall Variety Show, popular in Victorian and Edwardian times, where entertainers would perform music, songs, monologues, magic, dance and comedy.

It was a massive success, helped along by the audience who would dress up for the occasion in clothes of the era and thoroughly enjoy themselves joining in with the banter and singing - raising the roof for the finale which was always (and, still is!) *Down At The Old Bull and Bush*. By 1975, there was a long waiting list to be part of *The Good Old Days*, when over 24,000 people had their name down for a seat.

The first host in 1953 was Derek Guyler when the show was called *City Varieties* but, later that same year on the 20th July, the name was changed and Don Gemmell took over. However, after only three shows, he handed it to Leonard Sachs. A true professional Leonard had worked for Moss Empires touring all the major Variety Theatres and, his impact was so great on *The Good Old Days* that the original four episodes turned into thirty years!

We are so very fortunate that Barney chose the City Varieties for this long running popular television show which put the theatre 'on the map!' He revived *The Good Old Days* as a stage-only production five years later which ran until his death in 1991 when he suffered a stroke. He was 77 years old.

Many say that Barney went on to save the City Varieties for without *The Good Old Days*, both the television version and the stage version, the theatre would probably have gone the way so many others have in the name of progress.

Thank You Barney.

Peter Sandeman is awarded a Certificate of Achievement
by The Old Theatres Magazine
'In recognition of the huge contribution he has made to the theatre Industry over 25 years'

Photo left to right: David Aspinall, Caroline Fields, Peter Sandeman, Vernon Blades and Ivor Dykes at the unofficial hand-over! The official one took place on Sept 29th, 2013

In addition, Peter was given The Philip Windsor 'Spanner Award' 2013
'For outstanding services to theatre'
by Vernon Blades, Secretary of The Association of British Theatre Technicians Northnet

PETER SANDEMAN

Shadwell, Leeds

I was born and brought up in Cardiff and so my earliest memories of the *City Varieties* Music Hall are probably, as with most people, seeing it on BBC Television as the home of *The Good Old Days.*

That was until I came to Leeds in 1978 to work at the *Grand Theatre.* I soon got to know the brothers - Michael and Stanley Joseph who owned and ran the *City Varieties.* Then in the early 1980s I managed to get tickets for a tele-recording of the show.

When I arrived, I was bemused to find there were no television cameras. When everyone was seated Barney Colehan (producer and director of the show) came on stage to explain to the audience that due to an inter-union dispute, that evening's show would not be recorded. But, as we were there in our costumes and the cast was there, the show would be presented just for us.

Topping the bill that night was Ken Dodd. As it was no longer a tele-recording, I'll leave you to guess what time we left the *City Varieties*!

In 1987, Michael and Stanley Joseph put the *City Varieties* Music Hall up for sale. Councillor George Mudie (then leader of Leeds City Council and now MP for Leeds East) stepped forward to announce it would be bought for the benefit of the city. The sale, effected through the Leeds Grand Theatre & Opera House Ltd. went through in 1987. The venue was leased back to the Josephs so they could fulfill their pantomime commitment for the 1987/88 Christmas season.

Then in February 1988 when the Grand Theatre company took over the running of the *City Varieties*, I moved across from the *Grand Theatre* to the *City Varieties* to become General Manager. It was certainly a challenge to build the programme and the audiences to what they are now. At that time I was a one-man band operating out of the office on Swan Street. I realised I was going to need help and support so I immediately roped in family and friends and set up two groups which have proven to be vital elements of the success of the *City Varieties* - the Volunteers and The Friends of the *City Varieties.*

I will always be grateful to Councillors Elizabeth Nash (who gave me the opportunity), Bernard Atha CBE and Ronnie Feldman who all had a clear vision and the management and leadership skills needed to breathe new life into the venue and to establish the *City Varieties* as a premier venue for entertainment.

The first show I booked into the *City Varieties* was the 'ELO Experience'. On the first night it wasn't until we came to the interval that we realised the *City Varieties* was not equipped with any bar-bells to communicate to the audience the interval was nearly over. The next day I mentioned this in a call to Michael Joseph whose reaction was, "Oh yes, people would ask how long was left on the interval, to which we would reply - the show finishes in ten minutes!" So inviting was the Circle Bar that many members of the audience missed the second half of the show!

Back in 1988, I felt it was an obvious choice to include 'Music Hall' in the new programme, so I contacted Barney Colehan and together we re-staged *The Good Old Days,* which became a favourite with audiences, as did the pantomimes which I produced in house. Over the years there have been many changes and developments with the *City Varieties* going from strength to strength.

Long may it continue.

Photo by kind permission of Jean Brier

THE EXECUTIVE COMMITTEE
OF
THE FRIENDS OF THE CITY VARIETIES

From left to right:
Dot Foster, Frances Ingram (Secretary)
Doreen Driscoll (Membership Secretary) Don Foster (Chairman)
Peter Sandeman, Harry Fisher (Treasurer) Alan Pickett
Gail Sandeman, Caroline Fields, Marion Hopper (Members Welfare)

THE FRIENDS OF THE
CITY VARIETIES
MUSIC HALL

*This year is the 25th Anniversary of
The Friends of the City Varieties*

The Friends of the City Varieties was founded by Peter Sandeman in 1988 and registered as an independent charitable organisation. It has campaigned tirelessly over the years to fund the essential upkeep of the theatre.

In addition to the donation of £175,000 toward the recent refurbishment, their efforts over the years have also provided the venue with replacement auditorium seating, heating for the bars and hot drink machines.

In recognition of their contribution to the theatre, the circle bar has been named '**The Friends Circle Bar**'.

These funds have been raised through activities such as raffles, street markets, cash collections, stalls, charity performances, dining events and the operation of city centre charity shops. Their social events regularly include luncheons, quizzes, garden parties, theatre outings, museum and cinema visits as well as sail and shop trips to the continent.

If you are interested in joining this dedicated and sociable group of City Varieties supporters, please contact the Box Office on 0113 243 0808 or drop into reception in Swan Street and pick up an application form. Benefits of membership include priority booking, regular newsletters, discounts and special offers on selected shows, discounts on merchandise and exclusive Friends events.

*Friends of the City Varieties
Registered Charity number 1038435*

CITY VARIETIES
MUSIC HALL · LEEDS

With grateful thanks to everyone who contributed to this book

City Varieties Music Hall
Swan Street
Leeds
LS1 6LW
www.cityvarieties.co.uk
Box Office: 0113 243 0808

COUNCILLOR BERNARD P ATHA CBE

Civic Hall, Leeds

My life-long connection with the *City Varieties* started in the 1940s when I saw some of the country's best Music Hall Artistes, made some 'forbidden-by-parent' visits to see Phyllis Dixey, and later, seeing almost all of the broadcast *The Good Old Days* shows from the front row of the Circle, thanks to the friendship of the magical Joseph Brothers and Barney Colehan. Happy Memories.

Later, as Chairman of the Theatre, I worked with Peter Sandeman, an outstanding manager, who reduced the cost of the theatre, year on year. We owe him a deep debt of gratitude. His departure was our loss.

I remember saying to George Mudie, then Leader of the Council, that the *City Varieties* would never make a profit, unlike the *Grand Theatre*, but it was a unique asset in the cultural riches of the City of Leeds and should be saved. How far-seeing George was to purchase it. Would that we had the same courage and vision today. Long may the Varieties Music Hall reign as Queen of the Theatres. Long live 'The Friends' who have done so much to preserve this heritage.

Above: Bernard Atha with actress Liz Dawn

IT'S YOUR OWN, YOUR VERY OWN!
YOUR WORTHY CHAIRMAN OF *THE GOOD OLD DAYS*

Johnny Dennis recalls his Memories

In 1962, under the keen eye of Bernard Miles, I made my professional debut at London's Mermaid Theatre. Actor and manager, Brian Rix then took me on at the Whitehall Theatre in his famous farce company.

Eventually, I met a group of artistes and we started an 'old timer' music hall above a pub in Blackheath - we performed just at week-ends. Our only pay was the bus fare home!

As well as doing comic songs, I was asked to be Chairman and was awful at it. But, I was soon addicted by the fun in having contact with the audience. We were actors playing at it but, when we visited the famous Players Theatre, (underneath the arches at Charing Cross) we saw the experts at work - Barry Cryer, Clive Dunn and Sheila Bernette were amongst the stars.

When Barney Colehan cast his first show of *The Good Old Days* in 1953, the very first chairman was Don Gemmell, a Director of the Players. When Don eventually turned the BBC down he suggested Leonard Sachs.

Whilst Leonard was at *The Good Old Days*, I was gaining more experience as a Chairman and was soon touring overseas with the Players. Barney was approached by new Manager, Peter Sandeman, to produce a stage version of the show. He asked Leonard but he said no. He suggested me. And here I am, twenty-odd years later still banging the gavel there!

Barney was a pleasure to work with. He had worked with them all but was still charming and relaxed - that was, until you messed up. Then watch out! (Any little stage-craft I have I owe to him.)

The role of chairman, as I see it, is to warm up the audience, present the artistes in the best possible way and be ready to fill in when things go wrong (which is often) with the odd joke or song. It is a role to be enjoyed, but really it is an acting role and you must remain calm and confident and be able to 'ad lib' with your audience at all times. You may find it hard to believe but, in real life, I am shy and retiring!

Most of the things that go wrong the audience never notice but sometimes they do notice and, of course, find it greatly amusing - as long as they see you are in control.

Years ago I introduced a speciality act but he was still in his dressing room at the very top of the theatre and didn't hear my introduction. After repeating it, there was still no act, so I went into some 'gags'. The audience now knew something 'was up'. Then I heard the poor man come crashing down the back stairs with his props. I gave him time to get his breath and repeated the intro to even more laughter from the audience. He came on and never stood a chance. They roared at every dropped prop. It's a tough life on stage!

A lighter note was when my friend, Anita Harris, appeared there in her male attire role as Burlington Bertie. I introduced her and she looked terrific in her tail suit and tight trousers but, as she took one step, the 'flies' of the said trousers burst open (it was, in fact, a zip). She smiled and said, "I'll be back," (to much laughter) and I told some jokes before Anita called from the wings, "I'm ready".

We repeated the whole introduction again - only for her to get on stage - and the zip go again! (By this time the audience was crying with mirth). And when Anita finally appeared with heavy safety pins in position, they cheered! When she went off they were still roaring with laughter and, as luck would have it - the interval. What a night!

Many of the artistes who appear at the Varieties are in awe of the place - aware of those 'greats' who have played on it's famous stage. There are few theatres left of this stature.

The *City Varieties* has a soul...a heart...And long may it serve the public and thrill future artistes who will perform there. For more than twenty years, in spring and autumn, I have had the honour to be 'Mr. Chairman'. And it's all down to Leonard and Barney.

My thanks to Britain's OLD THEATRES magazine - Ed
Http://www.oldtheatres.co.uk

BARRY CRYER OBE
Harrow

Born in Leeds I am known as an entertainer and writer. I also sing a few songs and tell stories. I first played the *City Varieties* in 1956 whilst still at Leeds University studying English Literature. I emerged as BA Lit. (Failed). And now they've offered me an Honorary Doctorate - frankly, I'm astonished.

I played the *City Varieties* last year and to the audience, mentioned that I last played there in 1956 and proudly said, "They've asked me back."Although, that's not strictly true, as I've appeared in *The Good Old Days* several times throughout the years.

How did I come to be there? Well, Stanley & Michael Joseph (whose Father, Harry, owned the theatre) would go to see student shows at Leeds University and, if they liked somebody's act, they would offer them a week's work at the Varieties. One year they did so for Frankie Vaughan who was at the Leeds College of Art at the time.

I used to do a double act with Bernard Cribbins and, when we went on *The Good Old Days* we joked to producer Barney Colehan that he got three acts for the price of two, as we had both done a single spot each in the first half of the show before appearing together in the second half! We didn't care as working at the *City Varieties* was such an incredible experience, and still is. One of the two oldest Music Halls in the country.

May it live forever.

THE JOSEPH FAMILY

By Michael Joseph - Pool In Wharfedale, West Yorkshire - talking to the editor

My father, Harry Joseph came to Leeds in 1941 from London where he had a group of theatres in the South of England, including the *Lewisham Hippodrome* (3 seats more or less than *The Palladium*).

He was slowly selling off his theatres because of the bombing - which was really bad in the South. When the *Lewisham Hippodrome* was bombed in 1941 he felt it was time to give up and look for other theatres away from the onslaught.

Some friends told him about the *Empire Theatre* - a variety and repertory venue - for sale in Dewsbury. He decided to take a look.

They all met up when my Father arrived in Dewsbury. He was quite interested in buying it but decided to mull it over whilst they all had a meal. However his friends said, "We'll have to go into Leeds if you want something to eat as there's nowt much to do here in Dewsbury." (There wasn't at the time!)

After a meal in Leeds, to finish off the evening they popped into the *City Varieties'* Circle Bar for a drink. There was only one person in the bar - a little old lady who was sat quietly knitting in the corner. Out of politeness my father introduced himself and eventually discovered she was the owner! She also owned the *Theatre Royal* in Castleford.

My father got chatting to her and suddenly (almost jokingly), asked if she wanted to sell. To his absolute amazement she said, "Yes, if you like." My mother, Pearl didn't mind moving away from London as she wanted to escape the bombing. But, whilst my father moved up to Leeds almost immediately, she didn't move up until 1946 as we three children (Nita, Stanley and myself) were still at boarding school (out of London) and she didn't want to uproot us. When Nita left school she helped to

*Stanley Joseph (standing)
with Angela Agar seated.
Photograph kindly loaned by
Sylvia Thompson, Headingley, Leeds.*

run the Lewisham theatre after it was re-built, (It was badly bombed during the war and is now a supermarket.)

After leaving school I came up to Leeds to go straight into 'the business' with my father. Stanley went into the airforce and came out in 1945. He then joined me at the *City Varieties*. He died in 2008.

Nita married after the war in 1947 and has two children. She is now retired and still lives in London.

The general entertainment of the day in the mid 50s, in what we call 'Number Two' theatres around the country, was variety and revue and always included nudes. This kept theatres like ours alive and working. The girls would do the circuit going from theatre to theatre. Everyone called these girls 'strippers' but that is not correct as they didn't have any clothes on to strip off! And, they were banned from moving. The girls were 'discovered' already set up on stage in different poses. Sometimes they depicted a scene from history, a play or an event. When they changed poses either a gauze would be brought in or there would be a blackout on stage.

As well as the girls, our revue shows had a fine line up of comics, magicians, singers, speciality acts and dancers and the shows were well patronised. Eventually, the girls were replaced by more variety artistes. Barney Colehan came to us for *The Good Old Days* and the rest, as they say, is history. Later, we set up an entertainment agency for actors and variety performers. Called A.T.S. Casting this was one of the biggest theatrical agencies in the North. We represented thousands of artistes for film, television and stage. During the war years the *City Varieties* never closed and may we hope it never will.

14

KAY MELLOR OBE
Leeds, Yorkshire

Photograph by kind permission of www.kytephotography.co.uk

The *City Varieties* Music Hall theatre has been a part of the Mellor family life for generations. Year after year we've had family outings to see the pantomimes. We would collect as a family - sometimes there would be 16 of us with 4 generations - and we would have a wonderful night out, laughing, throwing sponges and generally having a fantastic time.

It's those images passed down from generation to generation and its rich theatrical tradition which has fuelled my daughter's and my grandchildren's love of theatre.

Gaynor's stage debut was on the boards of the *City Varieties*. She was only 16 years old when she played the lead role of 'Sharon Christmas' in an alternative Christmas pantomime, *The Electric Christmas Show*. The rest is history. She's played all over the world, from the West End to the US, and is currently playing Megan Macey in Emmerdale.

More recently, the *City Varieties* opened it's doors to me as a playwrite when Peter Sandeman invited me to workshop a new play, 'High Level Cleaning.' It's something I'm still working on but, the opportunity to explore the script was invaluable. I'm sure that, one day, the play will be performed in all its glory - thanks to the *City Varieties*.

JOHN THORPE MBE
Cyprus

Memories of the *City Varieties*? Two in particular. I, and a bunch of Leeds City Councillors, found myself on the front page of the Yorkshire Evening Post Newspaper - accused of 'queue jumping'. It was the Christmas recording of *The Good Old Days* and followed the successful 'Jeux San Frontiers' staged in Roundhay Park.

Barney Colehan was producer of both shows and invited members of the city council to the Christmas recording as a "thank you" for their co-operation in making the Roundhay Park event such a success.

I was invited as the Yorkshire Evening Post's then municipal correspondent. I thought nothing more about the event (although I did dress up as an Admiral of the Fleet) until I read the Boxing Day splash in the Yorkshire Evening Post. One of the eagle eyed members of the Yorkshire Evening Post news desk team, who had been on the waiting list for tickets for years, saw the councillors and myself on TV in prime seats and 'blew a gasket'. At the time the waiting list for tickets to the Christmas recording was something like 10 years. Hence the front page story. Was I embarrassed? No, quite chuffed really that I had got 'one up' on the great (and now late) Fred Willis whom, if I'm not having a 'senior moment' had his byline on the front page splash.

The other also involved my newspaper. Les Parkin, a Yorkshire Evening Post assistant editor, got a story about the brewer Whitbread wanting to buy the *City Varieties* from the Joseph brothers and turn it into a theme pub. It too was a front page splash in the Yorkshire Evening Post. Soon after lunchtime, when the paper hit the streets, Coun George Mudie, Labour leader of the city council phoned me.

George said, "John, there aren't many people you don't know. Having read the story about the *City Varieties* in tonight's Yorkshire Evening Post will you set up a meeting any place, anywhere, any time for me with Michael Joseph? I want to buy the *City Varieties* for the city. No way do I want it turned into a theme pub. We have to preserve it for the people of Leeds". I did as requested and the *City Varieties* was duly saved by George, now MP for East Leeds for the people of Leeds. Long may it remain in public ownership

Columnist and Feature Writer
The Yorkshire Evening Post 1969-2007

VALERIE JEAN MANN
Bradford

I remember when I was in my late teens going to the *City Varieties* with a group of friends. The boys decided they would book the front row to see the nudes, shock the girls in the group and have a laugh at our expense. But when we arrived at the theatre, to the girls delight, it was a Variety Show.

All went well until the mind reading act came on and he asked for a volunteer to be his assistant. Before I knew it, the boys had hoisted me onto the stage.

I had to place a blindfold on him and ask members of the audience to hold up different articles. Then I had to choose one and concentrate very hard on that particular item whilst holding his hand.

My thoughts would then be transferred to his and with great applause he would tell the audience what the item was.

Later on in life I became a magician (Mrs. Tipsy's Children's Show) and now I know how it is done, but of course I am sworn to secrecy. The last laugh was on the boys as I received a box of chocolates, which all the girls enjoyed!

Equity Branch Secretary
North & West Yorkshire Variety Branch

GERVASE PHINN
Tickhill, Doncaster

One afternoon just before Christmas, when I was ten, my father took me to see the pantomime at the Leeds *City Varieties*. We caught the train from Masborough Station in Rotherham and walked through the city crowded with shoppers. It was one of the few special occasions when it was just me and my Dad, no brothers or sister.

I had been in a theatre before but I had never been in a theatre as grand as the *City Varieties*. I was overwhelmed by the gaudy splendour of the building with the ornate painted plaster ceiling, red velvet covered seats, the great crimson curtains and the highly decorated arch above the stage. The floodlit stage, the sparkle and glitter, the chattering audience which surrounded me, the actors in their colourful costumes and outrageous wigs, intoxicated me. I

entered a different world. I visited this wonderful theatre a few more times in my childhood and, as a student in Leeds to the legendary *Good Old Days* (all dressed up as a toff) and recall the place with such affection.

The *City Varieties* is the oldest extant music hall in the country, an intimate, colourful and atmospheric little theatre, hidden between two arcades. All the greats have performed here: Charlie Chaplin and Houdini, Tommy Cooper and Marie Lloyd, Les Dawson and, of course, the legendary Ken Dodd who takes some persuading to leave the stage once he's started.

My favourite of all was the great Hylda Baker with her silent stooge, Cynthia, who managed to keep a face as rigid and serious as a death mask throughout her performance. Hylda Baker was a small woman (four foot, eleven inches) and characterised the fast-talking gossip. Her catchphrases, 'She knows, you know,' 'Be soon I said, be soon,' and 'You big girl's blouse' became household phrases. It is reputed that when she appeared at the *Stephen Joseph* Theatre in Scarborough, Noel Coward observed, after the performance he had "endured", that, "I would wring that woman's neck - if I could find it."

I appeared on that stage at the *City Varieties* myself in 2006 in my one-man show and spent the intermission leafing through the visitors' book fascinated by the many entries. Before my performance I stood on the empty stage looking down on the empty stalls and recalled a small boy sitting on a plush velvet seat with his father, his eyes (as we say in Yorkshire) 'like chapel hat pegs,' entering a magical world of the theatre.

Photo courtesy of Richard Murphy

BARBARA TAYLOR BRADFORD OBE

Manhattan

I have very fond memories of the *City Varieties* because my father used to take me there as a teenager growing up in Leeds. The theatre put on a lot of interesting plays, including the very gory 'Sweeney Todd' the Barber. Of course, my father took me to see other shows which were much more cheerful.

When I was a reporter on the Yorkshire Evening Post, I became a friend of one of the owners Stanley Joseph, who kindly showed me around the theatre which I found fascinating. I am so glad that the *City Varieties* is still going strong. May it last forever.

VINCENT HAYES MBE
London

I've always loved the *City Varieties* with its evocative interior. I first appeared there as 'Bob Cratchit' in 'A Christmas Carol'. My most recent experience was in a Music Hall and, it nearly became my last! I shared a dressing room with Johnny Dennis. As he left to chair the show, he threw a pair of underpants onto a light bulb by the artistes mirror to dry.

They not only dried, they caught fire...

When I returned to the dressing room after my spot, I was quickly overcome by the fumes! The rest of the cast were alerted by the strange smell and I was brought to by Jan Hunt giving me mouth to mouth resuscitation and a gentle massage. Can't be bad!

The adult pantomime with
supper included is splendid-Ed

Photo courtesy of Joanne Hayes, Brick Lane Music Hall

JOHN MORGAN
Scarcroft, Leeds

I began work at The Yorkshire Evening Post in 1945 and shall never forget my first day. My Editor, Mr. Henry Futrell told me to visit the *City Varieties* and the Leeds Empire and to write a report on both. He later gave me the *City Varieties* reviews as a weekly job. My brief was to write sixty words on such shows as, 'Strip, Strip, Hooray' and double that amount of words for the *The Empire*.

I saw the first house at the *City Varieties* and then had to make a mad dash across Briggate for the second house at *The Empire*.

I dare not tell my dear mother where I went each Monday. She was under the impression I was at school, studying Pitman's shorthand at Osmondthorpe Night School. Arriving home after that first visit to the *City Varieties* I spent hours in my bedroom writing notes, starting again, chewing fingernails, sweating profusely, and getting into a real panic. I submitted a 'book' to the editor who reduced it to one line! My mother said, "You're getting far too much homework at that night school!"

My family are deeply Catholic and when my mother discovered where I was going every Monday, she told my Editor that sending me to the 'VERTS' was a sin and threatened to withdraw my job at the paper. However, Mr. Futrell increased my wages from ten to twenty shillings. My Catholic mother then calmed down and said, "Ah, bless that wonderful man." The *City Varieties* was never regarded as 'sinful' again.

I covered the shows there until I was called up for National Service in the Air Force and saw some wonderful acts. I remember Jimmy James, Robb Wilton and Albert Modley, Donald Peers, Alan Jones and ' Steffani and his Silver Songsters' which is where Ronnie Ronalde, the brilliant whistler, first began his career.

I don't know when the *City Varieties* was built but do know that it was erected by Charles Thornton who also built Thornton's Arcade. It was little more than a concert room then. I've never lost my love of the *City Varieties* and I even appeared there on stage as MC in a charity show once. It was the thrill of a lifetime to stand where such famous performers had appeared. Long live the 'VERTS'.

P.s I am still a Catholic.
83 - Not Out!

JESS CONRAD OBE
KING RAT 2013

Sends "Every Best Wish With The Book" and says, "I Love That Theatre"

KENNY CANTOR
Kessingland, Suffolk

When I first went to the *City Varieties*, Harry Joseph (Father of Stanley and Michael) was there every night. So too was 'Pip' Pawson, the theatre manager - they were great days. I think I was in dressing nail number 6, just a bit higher than the fly floor. Jimmy Gay was also on the bill. He was a great comic who used to take snuff all the way through his act, he even threw some up in the air and followed it to the ground with his nose. At the end of his act he got a balloon out, blew it up, put some snuff in it and let it blow up his nose - it was so funny (at the time!)

In much earlier days, my Mum and Dad, Adele and Terry Cantor were working there and, during their act a rat came up one side of the stage, ran right across and disappeared down the other side - the audience went berserk. My dad told Harry Joseph who said, "What day is it Terry?" My dad said, "It's Tuesday." "That's funny," said Harry. "The rat doesn't normally come till Friday!"

It was Stanley and Michael who got us to bring back Pantomime after years of strip shows. It successfully ran for many years - I did the first four and, the last one I did, ran for 24 week - running longer than any other Pantomime in the country. It was brilliant. Wonderful days. I loved it - Oh, you are kind. I am proud to have been associated with the *City Varieties* and send many Congratulations to 'The Friends' for 25 years of success in keeping this wonderful and unique theatre alive and thriving.

KATHLEEN MARSH
Dewsbury

I took my friend Vera to the *City Varieties* about 20 years ago. She wouldn't admit it but she was slowly going deaf. She now wears a hearing aid at the age of 91.

We were sat in the front row and watching a variety show. But, when the great Leeds comedian Peter Wallis came on and started his routine, I realised she couldn't hear him as she began asking me what he had said. I kept telling her to 'shush' but, with everyone laughing at his jokes, she couldn't hear me either!

Well, he wasn't called Peter 'machine gun' Wallis for nothing and unless you listened you missed the punch line. His jokes really were 'quick fire'. At the end of one of his punch lines Vera asked again in a very loud voice what he'd said. I ignored her but she just kept asking.

The audience around us began to tell her to 'shush' too, which thoroughly embarrassed me. Peter must have overheard this commotion and soon realised what was going on. Quick as a flash, he bent right over the edge of the stage and said to her, "You'd better come up here love if we're going to do a double act!"

PAM AND COLIN FORD
Chaddesden, Derby

We've been going to the *City Varieties* for over 20 years and, during that time, have seen many wonderful shows in a beautiful theatre full of atmosphere. We especially enjoy the Music Hall Season, which we wouldn't miss for the world and often reflect on the names that have performed there that we would love to have seen.

Over the years, we've been privileged to see artistes such as Roy Hudd, Don Maclean, Bernie Clifton and James Casey and Eli Woods.

On one occasion, we saw Norman Collier and didn't realise it would be his last performance there. Such a wonderful person and an even bigger personality on stage than on television. He came into the bar afterwards and kept everyone entertained there too, so much so, that we didn't want to leave.

Roy Hudd also delighted in meeting the audience. Such a warm, jolly personality and so friendly. And, when James Casey and Eli Woods came into the bar after their show everyone recognised James but looked around for Eli. In a suit that fitted and without his 'gormless' expression, he completely blended into the crowd.

We missed our trips to the *City Varieties* whilst it was closed for the refurbishment, but that only made us appreciate it even more when it re-opened, now in its former splendour. What a relief that this theatre, like so many others, wasn't just abandoned and allowed to disappear. What a loss that would have been.

Pam and Colin are members of the Derby & Nottingham Music Hall Association and are staunch supporters of live theatre - Ed

TREVOR LEE
Annesley Woodhouse, Nottingham

To a supporter of live variety and someone with more than a passing interest in the history of Music Hall, the *City Varieties* can never be a forgotten theatre for me. To see it again, now looking splendid in its new suit, makes me think the legacy of the past will continue to be enjoyed by the patrons of future generations.

My memories of putting my bottom down in a stalls seat are not plentiful but special and etched in my mind, due largely to that extra slice of knowledge that I was waiting for a curtain to rise, revealing a stage that had been trodden by so many legends of Music Hall and Variety. The real thing, they were the heroes of the people. They knew their audience, who, in return gave their assurance that they knew and loved them.

Two pantomimes, two performances of television's *The Good Old Days* 30 years ago and recently, the weekend revivals of that production, provide the source of my memories. Not enough of my ' hard earned' through the box office to keep the mice in cheese I know, but that's my disappointment and I'm so pleased now to see the theatre has survived its own lean times.

Long live the *City Varieties* and long live the patrons who will be entertained with the presentations tailored for the 21st century in surroundings that shout, 'I represent theatre history, enjoy me!'

Trevor was a founding member of the Derby & Nottingham Music Hall Association - formed over 35 years ago - Ed

JEFF DENNIS
Leicestershire

I have a love of real-live performances and am from an era when we all went dancing to live bands when I loved to rock and roll all night. I loved watching 'Sunday Night at the London Palladium', the 'Black and White Minstrel Show', 'The Tiller Girls', and, of course, *The Good Old Days*.

I always wanted to go to Leeds to see a show - I loved the speciality acts and all the folk in period dress but, in those days, I was a young man working hard to support a family and never seemed to get around to it.

Then, it stopped being on telly and the years passed. I just had to forget all about it. Then, a few years ago, I saw an advert for a Music Hall Show at *The Palace Theatre* in Newark. It was only a 50 minute drive so we quickly booked and had a thoroughly enjoyable afternoon watching some very talented acts including a beautiful singer who wore splendid gowns - that was Caroline Fields, President of The Derby and Nottingham Music Hall Association.

At some point during the proceedings the MC mentioned that there was a large group in the audience from The Derby and Nottingham Music Hall Association who had come to support Caroline. I thought he must be joking. I never knew that such an organisation existed.

Once home, I was straight onto Google and lo and behold, yes, they really did exist. Within days I had made contact with the Secretary and made arrangements to attend their next monthly meeting. It was at that meeting I discovered that the *City Varieties* had just undergone a £9.9 million refurbishment and was running Music Hall Shows again.

I could not believe my luck. After all these years, I now had the chance to go and finally experience *The Good Old Days* for myself.

With the passage of time, I found myself doing less rock and roll and more ' old-time' dancing. In fact, my interest and love of all things Victorian had taken over. My business is restoring and selling Victorian fireplaces and I live in a Victorian rectory. All our furniture is antique and I love dressing in Victorian clothes.

So, off we went to the first available music hall show, feeling a little self-conscious walking around Leeds trying to find Swan Street in our Victorian outfits.

As soon as we walked into the building I fell in love with it. The beautiful ornate carvings, the warm mahogany panelling, the big Grandfather clock, the ambiance, the pleasant and enthusiastic staff. It was all I imagined and more. The intimacy of the theatre is overwhelming and I felt privileged to be in such a beautiful and unique place. It was saddened only by the thought of how many other exquisite places had been lost to 'progress'.

We settled down to watch from our box. We thought, "If we're going to do it, we'll do it properly." One great act followed another. Enjoying real genuine talent in close proximity was just as I had imagined all those years ago when watching it on TV. I had to pinch myself to convince myself it was all real. Here I was, actually sitting here in the *City Varieties* and joining in with all the audience. And, as if things couldn't get any better, we were awarded a prize for our Victorian costumes. We drove home full of joy and promised ourselves that we would attend every single Music Hall Show. And, we have.

Long live the Leeds *City Varieties* Music Hall Theatre and everything it stands for. May it be preserved for future generations.

Member of the Derby & Nottingham Music Hall Association

THE HOUGHTON WEAVERS
Bolton

My family was fortunate enough to get a television when I was about eleven or twelve years old. One of the shows that enthralled me more than any other was the long running *Good Old Days* show, hosted by the garrulous Leonard Sachs who enchanted me with his vocal dexterity. I sat spellbound watching Arthur Askey, Tessie O'Shea, Ken Dodd and roared with laughter at the one I thought funniest of all, Sandy Powell. These legends were walking in the footsteps of Charlie Chaplin, Harry Houdini and Marie Lloyd. Who would think that many years later I would be treading those very same boards! Would you believe that this Grade II listed building began life as the 'singing room' in the upstairs of a pub.

The Houghton Weavers became established in the North West of England because of our own television show that ran for six series. Then six series on Radio 2 and 3 albums with EMI, of all which gave us the opportunity to do some 'missionary work' in deepest Yorkshire. When our manager rang to say that we'd got a booking at one of entertainments most famous emporiums, I was ecstatic.

It was everything I'd dreamed of! The ceilings were too low, the dressing rooms were too small and smoke filled, the corridors too narrow, the stairs too steep... wonderful! We had to carry everything up the back stairs to the front of the stage, lift them some six feet in the air to access the rostrum and be careful not to see them roll back down because of the steep rake of the stage.

Once on stage the four of us would line up, and we soon realised that the ones on the outside could almost shake hands with the people in the adjacent boxes. The audiences were not polite like other theatres but felt it was their duty to join in the act. In other words, everything about the place screamed 'show business' and you know what? There's no business like it! I can't remember the number of times we've been on the billing of this wonderful shrine of entertainment but I pray we'll be coming back for many years to come.

And, that's some compliment coming from a Lancastrian.

Long live the *City Varieties*!

CHAS AND DAVE
London

We've had some great times at the *City Varieties* over the years. In fact, more years than we care to remember. And, we look forward to many more.

It's certainly looking in great shape since it's wonderful refurbishment - it's always been a joy to work there - but now, there's even somewhere to sit! The audiences are always tremendously appreciative and love joining in with our music, stories, banter and cockney humour. Maybe it's because they are northern folk or maybe it's the atmosphere of that special theatre. Whatever, it is - it works for us! We love it. Long may it reign as one of the most unique theatres in the Country and we hope folk recognise it for the special place it is.

THOUGHTS FROM THE GREEN ROOM

Life backstage can't be revealed
Because alas! My lips are sealed
So, all the juicy bits I hear
Some sights I see - Won't tell - No Fear!
There is a man who brings his birds
The feathered kind (I'm lost for words)
Hens and pigeons, geese and doves
J.D. Says, "Clean this up, loves"
And Roger with a mop and pail
Removes the 'splodges' without fail.
Artistes brings their dogs along
For me to mind whilst they're in song
Dora's 'Lottie' - Richards 'Barney'
'Jonty's' kissed the Heavenly Blarney.
Crosswords always go down well
And, if the answer we can't tell
In spite of efforts from us all
Our M.D. has been known to call
At Waterstone's to consult 'tomes'
Returning to dispel our moans
"We've no Hats left"- the old refrain
Is what I dread to hear again
There's so much more you'll never know
I cannot tell you either - So...
It's half time now and, "Where's the tea?"
"You've made some biscuits...Good old C"
Here's Peter with their cheques, he'll say,
"Tea and Biscuits? Mmm...I'll stay!"
It's time to sing the Bull and Bush
So, I'm off home before the rush!

CLARICE EARNSHAW
Gildersome, Morley

Clarice Earnshaw was initially a volunteer in the wardrobe department at the Grand Theatre where she first met Peter Sandeman. When Peter was transferred to the City Varieties and became General Manager, he and Barney Colehan decided to create a stage version of The Good Old Days after the BBC ceased to televise the programme. Peter asked Clarice to join him at the City Varieties. As a volunteer, she is still involved - well over 30 years service as a Dresser, Seamstress, Dog-handler,* Baker, Tea-maker and 'Confidante' to the stars - Ed

**('Lottie' - Dora Bryan's dog who always took a bow at the end of her performance.
'Barney' - Richard Gauntlett's doggie & 'Jonty' - Danny La Rue's doggie)*

DAVID AND SHIRLEY BUTTERFIELD

Rawdon, Leeds

In the late 60s, after several years of watching the programme, we finally got the opportunity to attend a recording of *The Good Old Days*. At the time I was a member of Aireborough Round Table and one of the other members was married to Rita Morris, a beautiful girl with a delightful singing voice, who regularly appeared on the show.

Because of the connection, we were able to side-step the considerable waiting list and so, a large party of us dressed up for the occasion. I recall that my outfit consisted mainly of a rather loud striped blazer and a straw boater.

We cannot for the life of us remember who else was in the cast, but it was Rita we had gone to see and hear. She often appeared on a swing above the audience and this was one of those occasions. It was quite breathtaking when the swing came right over our heads.

That evening, we entered fully into the spirit of the occasion, as the audience always did, with all the usual hearty singing, cheering and occasional catcalls.

The evening passed very quickly, a good measure of our enjoyment.

HELEN BAXTER

Wetherby

As a wee lass, my father's work brought us to Yorkshire from Scotland. That first year they took me to Lewis's to see Father Christmas where we queued for hours on winding concrete steps and then passed moving tableau.

We also went along to the *City Varieties* to see the pantomime. I was so excited I thought I would burst.

It was so magical and colourful. The scenery, the players, the slapstick comedy and the enthusiastic audience were all strange to me and I could only learn how to react to what was happening on stage by watching the audience.

I've never forgotten it. A wonderful memory.

DAVID CONWAY

Christchurch

I love playing the *City Varieties* and am always pleased to be invited back. It is like no other theatre and I've played most. It has a unique atmosphere and aura and, when on stage, you are aware of all the great names that have stood there before you.

On several occasions I was on the bill with the nudes. One I remember was the 'Leg Show' and starred Jackie Parker.

I would like to take this opportunity to wish The Friends of the *City Varieties* a long and happy future.

*David was one of
'The Three Monarchs' for many years- Ed*

DAVID HAIRYES

Leeds

Written by Nicholas Hairyes

My father David Hairyes, remembers going to the *City Varieties* many, many times and says he always had a wonderful time there.

He especially enjoyed being at the recordings of *The Good Old Days* and remembers seeing Morecambe and Wise, Les Dawson, Rod Hull, Pat Mooney and Peter Hudson to name a few.

He always went into the bar afterwards in the hope the cast would come in so he could say 'hello'. Sometimes they did and he met many greats artistes. He got to shake hands with the likes of Danny La Rue, Albert Modley, Reg Varney, Roy Castle and Ted Ray.

He was introduced to the Music Hall by his mother when they would travel to Leeds from Worksop. In later life he came to live in Leeds where, once again, he renewed his interest in the *City Varieties* Music Hall.

In 1966 he remembers seeing Phyllis Dixie when it cost only six old pence in the gallery, yet still afforded him a good view of the burlesque dancers.

Dad says it's the most welcoming and wonderful venue he has ever seen and his memories still linger on.

ANDY EASTWOOD
Christchurch

I have a special affection for the legendary *City Varieties* - not only for it's history but because it's a perfect theatre to work in. I've appeared there many times, but my fondest memory is of appearing in the unforgettable re-opening night with Doddy after the superb refurbishment.

The atmosphere is remarkable! Here's to your glorious future!

BOB TEBB
Adel, Leeds

As Chairman and Musical Director of Headingley Amateur Operatic Society, I have had the pleasure of performing in this wonderful old theatre. In 1981, we performed 'The Gondoliers' at the invitation of The Leeds Festival. In 1982, for a week, we presented 'Salad Days' with Norman Hudson and myself on two pianos to sell out houses. Then, in 1983, we performed 'The Boyfriend' with full orchestra to packed houses.

We were warmly received by Peter Sandeman, the Manager, and all the staff of the *City Varieties*, which is like no other theatre with it's own ambiance and fantastic atmosphere. Members of our Society also attended a performance of *The Good Old Days* - and everyone in costume. I will always have fond memories of my time spent performing at this wonderful and unique venue.

THE SEARCHERS

Frank Allen - London

At first it seemed odd - The Searchers appearing at this hallowed venue. All we knew about the *City Varieties* was that it was home of the television show *The Good Old Days*, a platform for artistes in period costume singing comical Cockney songs about cock linnets, furniture removal vans and a strange fellow called 'Burlington Bertie From Bow'.

But if that was the pop music of its day and was still being revived decades on then we, who were the pop stars of our era now enjoying our own revival, were simply an appropriate continuation of the status quo. A clever wag once said 'nostalgia is not what it used to be'. Not true. It always will be what it used to be.

The interior is impressive to an immense degree and it was so gratifying to see the results of the recent renovation which took place some time after we had already made three or four appearances there, which I might say were received with such enthusiasm that we looked forward to every return visit. The glamour of showbusiness however is so often a myth with the grandeur coming to an almighty halt as soon as one enters the backstage areas. The 'dressing cupboards' at the *City Varieties* (one size fits all) was legendary. I swear there were marks on the wall where someone had unsuccessfully tried to swing a cat.

I can only liken it to a hospital operation where one is obliged to strip and don a backless apron before surgery. It looks fine from the front but poke your head round the back and the glamour soon fades.

After the expensive but so worthwhile refurbishment, the most astonishing transformation was the appearance of six perfectly acceptable and spacious dressing rooms complete with modern conveniences which could have only been created by Merlin or any other competent magician. The old place had been a tardis all the time.

We have no special or amusing tales to tell about our times there except that we have loved every occasion we were given the chance to perform there.

The *City Varieties* is a unique and special place, which must be maintained for generations to come.

Photo of The Searchers by kind permission of Brian Crump

MICHAEL CARR

Bridgeway Street, London NW1

This is both a very sad story in part and also one that changed my Stage Name from Malcolm Carmichael to Michael Carr.

As a young popular singer from Hull just starting out in Variety, I was very much looking forward to my week at the *City Varieties*, which was headlined by 'Jane' the stripper who came to fame by being the subject of the famous Daily Mirror strip cartoon. She was also a very talented stage performer who had appeared at the theatre many times before. I remember arriving at the theatre on the Monday for band call to see my name right across the bottom of the bill, which was just slightly larger than the printer's name.

To say the least, I was slightly peeved about the situation and rang my agent straight away, who's immediate response was, "Well, with a name as long as yours it was the only place they could fit it in! Look, why don't you forget the Malcolm, reverse the Carmichael and take the name Michael Carr?" I took his advice and was never bottom of the bill again.

That week I also shared a dressing room with a great musical performer named Tommy Elliott, a wonderful elderly gentlemen who had been part of a great family act. They had toured in Variety for many years - known as The Musical Elliotts. We had some great laughs that week and I learnt a lot from what's known in the business as a real 'Pro'.

How he had performed that week I will never know as it was not until after the last show on Saturday night and we were having a drink together at the bar, when he told me that, he and his wife had been travelling down the M1 motorway only a couple of weeks before when the car had broken down. So they pulled onto the hard shoulder to see what was wrong and, as she stepped out of the car, a large lorry hit her and killed her immediately. It was then he really wept and it truly brought home the saying "The Show Must Go On". For, the week we had just done they should have been performing together. What a guy, eh?

WEYLAND AND YVONNE ROBERTS

Holmfirth

It was only in our retirement that we started to visit the *City Varieties* on a regular basis. We loved discovering and learning about the theatre and found it to be a real historical gem. A building of beauty to be treasured and preserved.

The shows, of course, are excellent but our lasting memories are of the warm welcome from 'The Friends' of the theatre, notably Don and Dot Foster, Peter and Gail Sandeman and Caroline Fields and her husband John.

Over the last decade the *City Varieties* has given us many, many hours of pleasure and so, in an attempt to 'put something back', we decided to support the theatre financially. We did this initially by making monthly gift-aided donations and then, when the opportunity arose, we sponsored a Box. So, next time you are in the theatre please pop into Box D and read the message we have put there for you.

BROWNIE DENE

Seymour House, Tavistock Place, London

I directed pantomime at the *City Varieties* for eight years from 1980. I loved working in that fine theatre but the small stage was a challenge.

Once when I was directing 'Cinderella' we were using real ponies but couldn't get them up the steps quietly to the stage. They made such a racket - we knew it would spoil the surprise for the audience as they would be able to hear them coming. When I mentioned this to stage manager Wally, he just said, "I'll sort it. Just wait and see". So I did.

All the way through dress rehearsal, I waited anxiously for their entrance. Then, led by two small boys, on came the ponies pulling Cinderella's coach.

How had he got them up the steps so quietly? Well, Wally had put each of their hooves into padded socks - removing them when the ponies were in the wings waiting to go on stage. Priceless.

Another memory is of the BBC doing a recording of *The Good Old Days*. Well, they had the most wonderful modern lighting equipment. There was this type of light and that type of light - you name it, they had it. The *City Varieties* only had one follow spot which ran from above the 'gods'. It was fine for the panto but, when I saw the ones the BBC had brought in I was envious and hoped they would leave me one. I jokingly tried to smuggle one away. "You won't miss one, will you?" I asked a BBC technician. "No, not at all, all yours" he laughed.

However, Ken Platt, the lovely warm comic who was with us for five years (known as Kenny Cucumber) saw me pretending to struggle with the light and asked if he could help. A different BBC lighting technician then saw us and came to help too. "Where do you want it?" he asked seriously. I was tempted to say, "In my dressing room," but just mumbled something about it almost falling over. I don't think he believed me and thought I was going off with it for real. Perish the thought!!

A Ratling and Past Queen Ratling - female equivalent of The Grand Order of Water Rats

NORMAN TAYLOR

Shadwell Lane, Leeds 17

I shall never forget my young days as a variety artiste. I worked every theatre in England including the *City Varieties.* You couldn't forget the *City Varieties* as you could only get off one side of the stage. I had learned how to play several brass instruments and, at 14, joined an act called 'The Four Blue Pages'.

Then I went into the army and was enrolled in the concert Party, 'Stars In Battledress' which was formed by Colonel Basil Brown, Major Bill Alexander and Captain George Black to keep morale high in the troops. On being demobbed, I formed an act called 'Tike and Del' and, in the forties was back working at the *City Varieties*. We also worked Leeds *Empire*. We were a talented act of singers and musicians.

This is my one and only photograph of me when I was in 'The Four Blue Pages' (We dressed in blue page-boy outfits) and topped the bill at the *City Varieties*.

NORMAN TAYLOR

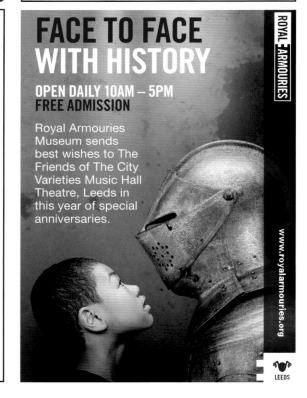

WYN CALVIN MBE

Cardiff

One of the joys of appearing at the *City Varieties* is its unique sense of intimacy (and I've always loved a bit of the intimate!) A performer can embrace the entire audience with a smile, a grin or a quick quip.

The ancient theatre builders knew how to design a venue which allowed every patron, wherever they sat, to feel in-touch with the performance - and, every artiste to experience the closeness of contact.

Another of the *City Varieties* interests has been the wide geographical range from which audiences travel to enjoy the specialness of the atmosphere and colour in which the entertainment is presented. One Saturday evening, during one of my appearances, I was surprised, if not astounded, to be greeted by a large section of the audience who had travelled from Holyhead on the Welsh Island of Anglesey - overseas visitors almost! A sing-a-long has always been a popular feature of the *City Varieties* performances and the singing that night was double-forte. It almost shifted the ancient rafters.

Wyn is a past king Rat of The Grand Order of Water Rats.
He is also a member of the Variety Club of Great Britain.
To date he has had 68 years in Showbusiness.

PETER AND FLOSS WHITE
Chislehurst, Kent

Our first visit came all a rush when the committee of The British Music Hall Society said, 'Lets have a visit to the *City Varieties* and make a week-end of it. We can stay at the Hilton'. That's when things started to go wrong. A fifty odd seater coach was booked, as were the tickets for the third great season of the Music Hall, which ran from 5th October to the 4th November, 1989. Not forgetting the fish and chip supper reserved across at the famous Nash's Tudor Restaurant in Merrion Street with overnight accommodation at the Hilton.

We set off but the driver took a wrong turning out of London. We think he had Leeds Castle in Kent on his mind instead of Leeds up in Yorkshire. Then, when we got back on track we broke down on the motorway. By now the fish and chip supper was looking doubtful. Finally a replacement coach arrived. Then the drivers had a committee meeting and argued about who was going to take us to Leeds. On our way again finally arriving at the Hilton, we had nowhere to park due to road works. Checking in at the hotel we discovered we were all on the upper floors and with some of our party fearful of using lifts, had a long haul up the stairs.

A visit to Nash's is an experience in itself, and at last we arrived at the restaurant. However, we discovered that because of our lateness they had let our tables. The helpful staff rushed around and eventually we were seated and enjoyed our long awaited supper of fish and chips.

We arrived at the *City Varieties* tired and exhausted but seated just in time. It was 'The Third Great Season of Music Hall', starring Chairman Johnny Dennis, Jean Pearce Dancers, Sheila Bernette, Duo Gavito, Deryk Parkin & Graham Richards, Kenneth McKellar, Bernie Clifton and Bubble Bee - a fantastic line up, enjoyed by us all and well worth the problems encountered on our trip there.

Peter and Floss are Members of
The British Music Hall Society

DAVID AND SUE ASPINALL
Bromley Cross, Bolton, Lancashire

It was Good Friday in the early 1970's. Where we lived - in Bolton, Lancashire - was 'closed'. Few shops open and entertainment nil.

We decided to cross the Pennines to Leeds. Shops open and so was the *City Varieties*. We had never been in the theatre before but had seen it many times on television. "How exciting," we thought and decided to see if we could get in. "Could I buy three tickets," I asked (My mother-in-law was with us.)

Yes, I could...three of the best seats in the circle. Wonderful atmosphere, but smaller than it looked on television. The standard of the show was indicative of the audience size of about thirty people. Some were the 'dirty mac brigade' and yes, we soon realised it was a strip show! I got good mileage from informing friends and relatives that I had taken my mother-in-law to a strip show in Leeds on a GOOD FRIDAY!

GEOFF QUIBBLE
Heanor, Derby

As a City Varieties theatre volunteer and 'Friend' of the theatre I arrived early, together with 'Your Worthy Chairman', Johnny Dennis for band-call on Friday 14th April, 2000 as part of the Music Hall season. The artistes Peter John, Tony Peers, Caroline Fields and David Conway all took their rehearsals with the band but the top of the bill, Russ Conway, had not been well and returned to his hotel.

The cast had all gone out or were backstage and I was completely alone in the stalls area of the auditorium when suddenly Russ Conway appeared on stage and, unaware I was there, proceeded to play the piano. He played several of his hit tunes much to my amazement and delight. I considered this to be a personal performance just for me and an occasion I will never forget.

I was later to learn the piano was new to Russ and unfamiliar so he had come to have a try-out and warm up his fingers.

It was a magical time in a wonderful theatre.

JOYCE CROWTHER
Leeds

Brian Halliday, Jim Ripley and I went to the *Grand Theatre* one night as we often did. Whilst in the bar we saw Peter Sandeman who said, "I've seen you all here before. How come you never come to my theatre?" "Your theatre? Which is that?" we asked in unison. "The *City Varieties*," Peter said. We promised to go and, as none of us had been there for years, the three of us went the following week. The two front rows had a sprinkling of people. We three had a box each. There was no-one else there.

"I need to do more for this theatre,"Peter said, and told us of an idea he'd had to form a 'Friends' group. So, form it we did. Brian became Chairman, Jim the Treasurer and I took the role of Membership Secretary.

Then came the hard part - getting other members to join us. We advertised for members and it soon took off. We started selling ice-cream and, in fact, did everything we could to get the ball rolling to raise money and to get folk interested in the theatre. Slowly it worked.

We held a grand raffle with a large TV for a prize. The monies from all our efforts went towards providing fires for the two bars and other improvements.

One spectacular event was a flower show in the auditorium and another, even better event, was when we three asked all our flower arranging friends to stage a variety show one Saturday evening and to do flowers to dress the stage. The best thing about this was the hundreds of people queuing up the Headrow to get in, and all of them dressed in their finery.

It was breathtaking and we organisers just had to go out to see the massive queue. We couldn't believe that we three and the flower arrangers had managed to pull this off so well.

That was the start of 'The Friends' and the following we have today!

Long live the *City Varieties*.

A founder member of ' The Friends'
of the City Varieties

BERNICE MATTHEWS
Scholes, Nr. Leeds

I love going to see the shows at the *City Varieties*. First my Mum took me and now I go with my boyfriend. We see all types of shows, the Music Hall, the comics and musical stars like Elkie Brooks (whom I love). We always make a night of it. We usually go for a drink first and then a meal afterwards. A great night out. I love that gem of a theatre.

JEAN AUTY
Barney's Secretary 1949-1956

The Good Old Days started in 1953 and we had some amazing people in the show - Rob Wilton who did the fireman sketch, "What do you mean it's GONE OUT? Can't you keep it going 'til I get there?"

Gracie Fields who felt she had made a mistake signing the contract as she didn't regard herself as Old Tyme Music Hall but was, by Barney, eventually persuaded to do the show and was brilliant. Ken Dodd, Hylda Baker and a very young soprano Mary Millar - Hyacinth Bucket's sister Rose - also came to perform.

We only had three cameras so we had to explain to the local theatrical societies, who were invited along as part of the audience, that we would only be able to film a few people in costume but they said they didn't mind and would like to dress up anyway and, that's how it all began.

The first Chairman was actor Derek Guyler reminiscing about the Music Hall but then Barney visited *The Players Theatre* in London and changed the format. We even 'borrowed' a few of their chairmen, Archie Gemmell, Robin Hunter and Leonard Sachs - who stayed!

I left Leeds in 1956 to move to London as my husband Jack Auty was climbing the BBC ladder and I was more important as Mrs Auty than Barney's Secretary it seemed. Anyway, we had 1st class rail travel to London.

Dear Dorothy Bickerdyke took over my job and stayed with Barney for the next 30 years. I lived in Harpenden and had six children.

THE WORLD FAMOUS CITY VARIETIES
POSTERS

The Book of Memories salaciously presents -
courtesy of Leeds Library & Information Service
www.leodis.net/playbills

HI! YA GALS
starts Monday December 19th 1960. Stars Gordon Peters and Jack Platts

STRIPPINGLY SAUCY
from Monday December 13th 1954. Colin Robins is bottom of the bill

SPREAD THE GOOD NUDES
beginning Monday April 29th 1963. Colin Robins is now second joint top.
Also features The Six Jean Pearce Dancers - Jean is the mother of comedian Billy Pearce

The Poster from Monday October 28th, 1912 (on page 45) is the oldest I could find -
101 years old. The Proprietor and Licensee was Fred. W. Wood of
13, Bishopgate Street, Leeds. The Manager was Albert Whiteman

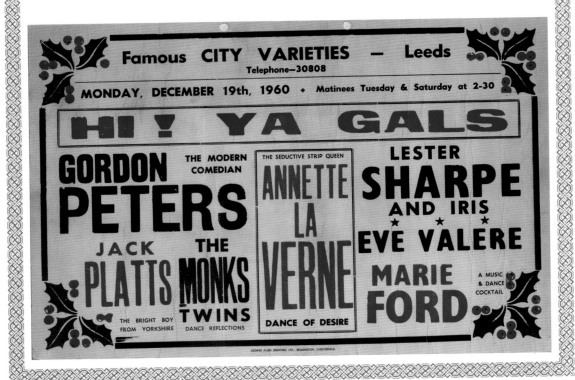

CITY VARIETIES

LEEDS
TEL. 30808/9

Manager & Licensee: PIP PAWSON, 25 Moynihan House, The Flats, Leeds 9

Box Office Open Daily

6.15 • Week commencing MONDAY, DEC. 13th • **8.15**

1954

MATINEES TUESDAY and SATURDAY at 2.30

THIS IS A 'HOT' SHOW - IT'S SO

'STRIPPINGLY SAUCY'

WITH

TED DWYER
HUMOROUSLY YOURS

GEDDES BROS.
PUTTING ON AIRS

HARGREAVES AND RUSSELL
MAN-MAID MUSIC

KARDOMA
HE FILLS THE STAGE WITH FLAGS

IRIS POLIAKOVA (BODY BEAUTIFUL)
THE BEAUTIFUL
BALLET DANCING NUDE
WITH HER
STARTLING NEW POSES

GLORIA AND GAY
BRING ON THE DANCING GIRLS

COLIN ROBINS
VERSATILE IMPRESSIONIST

WILLSONS. PRINTERS, NOTTINGHAM

BLONDIE 'GODIVA' HAIGH

Essex

I have been a lady ratling for over twenty years and had almost forgotten about my years as a dancer until I saw your article in The British Music Hall's 'The Call Boy' magazine asking for memories.

My first visit to the *City Varieties* was as a dancer when I was just 15. In those days there was a theatre, (usually two or three) in every town and I worked them all. I worked for months at a time but every tour would include the *City Varieties*. I was then in a three-handed act with the male impersonator Billie Roache and we did comedy, dance and instrumentals when these shows were called Variety.

I toured for years as a dancer. However, all this came to a gradual end when nudity became popular and, I joined the club so to speak. I became 'Blondie' Haigh, after first riding around Piccadilly in the nude for publicity, for the new all girl show, 'Godiva Rides Again'. This ran for a very long time, years in fact, and went to the *City Varieties* many, many times. The 'Godiva' ride around Piccadilly hit all the headlines and my work changed a lot as I became the top of the bill and was known as 'The Nude Who is Always In The News'.

We would do a week at a time at the theatre and always played to packed houses. We began on Monday with matinees every Tuesday and Saturday. Sometimes, we performed three shows a day at 2.30, 6.15 and 8.15.

Whilst I was billed as 'The Striptease Queen with the Fabulous figure', we 'Striptease Girls' didn't actually strip. We were nude, but were not allowed to move. The Manager, Pip Pawson, insisted we wore dressing gowns around the theatre until we were about to step on stage.

As you can imagine the theatre has many happy memories for me, as it will for most pros I expect. Also some funny memories - the stage was so small compared to other theatres, we always had a laugh on first nights (and, usually every night thereafter), trying to cram 6 or 8 dancers and a whole show onto such a tiny stage - it was, for us, the smallest stage of all the theatres we toured on the circuit. Nevertheless, it was always very cosy and had the best atmosphere. We all loved it there and had a marvellous time. It is a wonderful theatre. Long may it continue.

Jeri 'Blondie' Haigh with a mannequin

COLIN ROBINS
Barnsley

My first memory of the *City Varieties* goes back to the mid-fifties when as a young professional entertainer, I played a week on a variety bill there called 'Bare Facts of 1955'.

I had recently been demobbed from the RAF after serving my two year's National Service and was anxious to pursue a career on the stage. London agent Don Ross had seen me working in a show at the Pavilion in Redcar on the north east coast and contacted me offering a weeks' variety. I remember to this day arriving at the theatre at 10.30am on the Monday morning to take my 'band call' feeling somewhat nervous, especially as I had been told by numerous 'old pro's' to watch how the other artistes rehearsed with the pit band. They said to try and look as if you were quite used to rehearsing with the musicians and not to let them know that this was your first touring 'variety' date.

They told me to be sure that I had a music part for every instrument and that each part should be in a separate folder because, if there was one missing, the Musical Director would write one out for you and charge you for it!

There were eight acts on the bill including two 'strippers'. The opening dance act and the comic both did a couple of spots - one in each half - and the show ran twice nightly from Monday to Saturday, with two matinees. In those days, I was performing a vocal and impressionist act.

The owner of the theatre Harry Joseph, was a big bald-headed amiable man who was very rarely seen without a big cigar between his lips. 'Pip' Pawson was the theatre manager and Harry Burgoyne the stage manager. I have every reason to be grateful to big Harry Joseph because later I found out he had sent a highly complimentary report to my agent Don Ross about my act which, I have no doubt, helped me to establish myself on the variety theatre circuit. Over the next few years, I made regular appearances at the *City Varieties* both as a single act and later with my wife Angie Dean and will always cherish the memories I have of that wonderful old theatre.

GORDON PETERS
Surbiton

I have loved performing at the City Varieties over many, many years and send all my good wishes to this special venue and to all who have and who will entertain in the future in this unique theatre. My wonderful accompanist David Carter also sends his best wishes.

24-4-63

The Famous CITY VARIETIES - Leeds

TELEPHONE—30808

Week Commencing MONDAY, APRIL 29th, 1963

6-15 — TWICE NIGHTLY — 8-15

Matinees—Tuesday and Saturday at 2-30

SPREAD THE GOOD NUDES

LARRY MARSH ★ COLIN ROBINS

THE SIX JEAN PEARCE DANCERS

BILLIE WYNER

THE GAY BELLES

MURRAY SMITH

ANGIE DEAN

From the Night Clubs of Paris, Brussels and London

JEAN ROTHMAN

THE DARING STRIP-TEASE QUEEN

Printed by George Allen (Printers) Limited, Heywood Street, Brimington, Near Chesterfield.

VARIETIES

TOP OF BRIGGATE AND UPPERHEAD ROW, LEEDS.

Proprietor and Licensee: FRED. W. WOOD, 13, Bishopgate Street, Leeds.   Telephone 3170 Central.
Telegrams: "CITY VARIETIES, LEEDS."
Manager: ALBERT WHITEMAN.   Assistant Manager: BERNARD ARMSTRONG.

MONDAY, OCT. 28th, 1912

AND TWICE NIGHTLY DURING THE WEEK.

THE POPULAR ACTOR,

MR. SINCLAIR NEILL

And his London Company, including **Miss ALICE MILLER**, IN THE GREAT COMEDY,

DAVID GARRICK

CASTE.

David Garrick ... ... SINCLAIR NEILL	Alderman ...	... BASIL DYNE
Mr. Brown ... ... RUSSELL BARRY	Mrs. Brown ...	... JESSIE MELVILLE
Ada ...	... ALICE MILLER	

SCENE ... ALDERMANS HOUSE.   SPECIAL SCENERY AND EFFECTS.

LILY ARTHUR

Vocal Comedienne and Dancer

HARD LUCK BILL

Cowboy Comedy. depicted by the Variescope

MELT & BRAY

COMEDIANS

TWO COUNTEES

HUMORISTS AND HARMONIZING DUETTISTS

☞ JACK EDGE ☜

The New Star Comedian

☞ BAGGED ☜

Depicted by the Variescope

HENRY D. ADAMS

ENGLAND'S GREATEST JUGGLER

DAY PERFORMANCE EVERY WEDNESDAY

Doors open at 2, commence at 2-30.   ALL ARTISTES APPEAR SAME AS EVENING.

FRED. R. SPARK & SON, City Printing Works, Cookridge Street, Leeds

TREVOR BELL
Cornwall - formerly Leeds

Reminiscences? Must be getting on! It has been a pleasure thinking back to the *City Varieties* which, together with Whitelocks, was one of the essential experiences we all insisted upon on giving to visitors and whoever turned up at the time I was a Gregory Fellow at Leeds University.

That was an important time at Leeds College of Art when Harry Thubron, Ricky Atkinson and Tom Hudson were revolutionising the British art school system strongly supported by John Wood who was in charge of adult education in the city and, inevitably, the *City Varieties* was visited by many of the country's leading artists.

I know that everyone just loved the place which, at that time, was not a TV star but, a seedy hall. However, the atmosphere was perfect for the lovely sense of timelessness and related in our minds to the glamour of Lautrec and Belle Epoque but also, with a British feeling more to do with Sickert, good old pubs and Leeds at its best.

What a joy it was.

I wonder if the old acts such as the comedian with the rubber trombone or, when the law insisted that 'poses' must be stationary, or the tassel dancers - but, I will come to that- still featured when the place became so well-known?

The law, to prevent 'poses' moving, led to the wild invention of a moveable track on which the lady was 'posed' and then wheeled out over the orchestra. That solution did not last long due to the lady wobbling on it and having a fit of the giggles as she was fast advancing towards the audience.

She was then trundled back up just before the end of the track ran out, giving us all the added treat of the multiple movement of a mountain range, which added even more fun to the evening.

The bar was worth a visit on it's own and a gang of young men (us) would head up there and enjoy the show either from that vantage point or designate a chap to rush in and tell us when the strippers were on, which brings me to MISS BEVERLY.

Her performance was outstanding as she was a tassel dancer who had amazing control and, with a tassel on each, could make them rotate singly or together and what was even more amazing she had tassels attached to her rear and could get all four rotating in every way.

On one particular night it was so good we just had to invite her up to the bar in the interval for a drink and, to our absolute delight - SHE CAME!!

To transfer such a phenomena from the stage to real life (and she was a real 'a-l-l-o b-o-y-s'), we became totally out of our depth offering drinks and waited for the floor to open up. We can't quite remember how the evening ended, suffice to say, this really was a wonderful time in our lives.

Trevor is an Artiste. The Gregory Fellowship was set up by Peter Gregory to support Painters, Poets, Sculptors and Musicians

DAVID SMITH
Liversedge

I probably have the best seat in the house, sitting immediately in front of the stage, and have been privileged to see so many world class entertainers close up for the last 25 years.

The magic of Paul Daniels, Ali Bongo and Geoffrey Durham. Comedians like Larry Grayson, Peter Goodwright, Peter Wallis, Roy Hudd. Stars like Barbara Windsor and Danny La Rue. Singers such as Kenneth McKellar, Eartha Kitt and Marion Montgomery. Ventriloquists like the brilliant Ray Alan, John Bouchier, Keith Harris and so many more.

For many years the entire company of *The Good Old Days* would walk over to Nash's fish and chip restaurant between Saturday shows and the sight of the Beverley Sisters in matching fur coats stopping the traffic on the Headrow was a sight to see. Eartha Kitt was less than impressed with her dressing room until it was pointed out that it had been Charlie Chaplin's dressing room when he worked at the theatre.

Clive Dunn was a lovely man who presented me with a selection of Edwardian bow ties after the final show and, keeping us laughing long after the curtain had fallen, were John Inman and Bernard Cribbins, true variety artistes. Danny La Rue would bring the house down, whilst I was clearing feathers from the piano! Old timers like Dora Bryan and Margery Manners brought a touch of true Music Hall and Hinge and Bracket drew the audiences into their 'boudoir' with real style.

Sadly, many of these great artistes have passed on and we miss artistes like Frank Carson, Russ Conway, Ken Goodwin, Ted Rogers, Danny La Rue, Ray Alan, Norman Collier, Peter Wallis and Neville King.

Gone but not forgotten. Just a brief glimpse of the many stories that could be told. They have all been part of that great vision of our original Producer Barney Colehan, a true gentleman. Luckily there are artistes who still provide great Music Hall and Peter John, Richard Gauntlet, Judith Hibbert, Caroline Fields and many others keep the *Good Old Days* flag flying and playing to appreciative audiences who travel many miles to see the show. Long may it continue.

Tales from the Green Room are many. Before the recent multi-million pound refurbishment of the *City Varieties*, the Green Room, a place where the company could relax, was immediately behind the stage. Adjacent to that was the number 1 dressing room. Most 'Top of the Bills' kept an open door and joined the rest of the cast for a cup of tea during the interval.

Reminiscences were usually the main topic of conversation and we had many wonderful moments listening to tales from the 'business'. The fun in the Green Room often spilled over into the second half and I could sometimes hear the hilarity from out front.

Magic tricks from Paul Daniels, Danny La Rue's frantic costume changes, Larry Grayson's "Shut that Door" (Yes, he said it 'off stage' as much as on). Frank Carson's "It's the way I tell 'em," Frankie Vaughan practicing his high kicks, Barbara Windsor and Eartha Kitt - laughs a plenty. It was all part of the great joy and history of *The Good Old Days*.

We've seen them all - Great Memories!

Musical Director of The Good Old Days
1989 - present

THE POTATO ROOM PLAYERS

Stuart Woolf - Leeds

It was in the late 1980's when I was approached by the then Manager of the *City Varieties*, Peter Sandeman. The brief was simple - he wanted an amatuer musical theatre company to be resident at the theatre. I was to pick the cream of local amateurs and present slightly off-beat shows. I agreed to do just one show as a trial and we selected 'Lock Up Your Daughters'. It was a huge success and *The Potato Room Players* was born. I couldn't resist doing a second show 'Cabaret' and this was quickly followed by the regional amateur premiere of 'La Cage aux Folles'. By the time *The Potato Room Players* closed we had performed 'La Cage' six times.

We went from strength to strength. We started with one show a year and progressed to presenting two. We used different artistes in our productions, but the rule was always the same. Go for quality. Our choice of shows was enormously varied, from 'Sweet Charity' to 'Oliver' and 'Fiddler on the Roof' to 'Damn Yankees'. We received tremendous support from the city and always had a civic night, which was attended by the Lord Mayor of Leeds and City councillors.

Many professional artistes saw our shows. Both Jason Donovan and Billy Pearce came to see Lionel Bart's 'Blitz' and Matthew Kelly was a guest on video in 'Return to the Forbidden Planet'. *The Potato Room Players* believed that the line between amateur and professional theatre should be blurred and, with this in mind, we invited Danny La Rue to star in our production of 'La Cage aux Folles'. This was an unprecedented success with tickets selling out well before opening night.

Another production of note was ' Jolson'. We were one of only two UK amateur companies granted a license for the show, and this only served to cement our reputation of being ground-breaking and original.

We never lost sight of our raison d'etre which was to raise money for the *City Varieties*. During our tenure we donated around £60,000 to the theatre's upkeep. However, as time progressed our ticket prices couldn't keep pace with the escalating costs we were facing. When the theatre closed for refurbishment, it was decided to call it a day. We look back on the 20 years we were in existence with pride on a job well done.

Photograph - Danny La Rue and Pauline Woolf taken in the Circle Bar

ELKIE BROOKS
Devon

I have played the *City Varieties* a good few times over the years and it really is a unique and special theatre to perform in. It is often difficult to remember certain venues when you are constantly on tour, but this Music Hall really is different. It leaves such a lasting impression on both the performer and the audiences alike with it's beautiful shape and decoration. It also has a special warmth about it, as if the sheer fabric of the building is holding on to the memories of those wonderful stars who have gone before.

Whilst I love performing there, it has one heck of a rake on that stage, so I always have to bring the appropriate stage shoes!

Since the renovation the theatre has become even more glorious and reminiscent of its Music Hall days. It is a delight every time I visit Leeds and look forward to my next performance at the *City Varieties*.

Congratulations to ' The Friends' on 25 years of success.

NEVILLE KING 1928 - 2009

Cropwell Butler , Derbyshire

I was doing a mid-day matinee for comedian Les Wilson and promoter Brian Walker at Derby Assembly Rooms. Les was the compere and also on the bill was Neville King, Lizzie Wiggins, Dick Van Winkle and myself, Caroline Fields.

The curtain had already gone up but there was no sign of Neville. He'd missed band call but then his wife Joan, rang to say that Neville was on his way. They were due to come back from holiday the previous day but their plane had been delayed so had arrived home only a few hours earlier. He arrived in a panic during the interval so it was agreed that, to give him time to change and to ' warm ' em up', I would go on and do a 10 minute sing-a-long spot. I came off stage and stayed in the wings to watch as Neville went on. He took to the stage with his case and, after a bit of banter with the 'Old Boy' inside the case (The usual, "let me out, let me out," routine) Neville opened the case to get the 'Old Boy' out.

I could see the surprise on his face - more like horror - for a brief moment and we both looked down to the floor of the stage to see that inside the case was socks, pants and towels - but no doll!

He'd forgotten to put the doll back in after using the case on holiday. If you've ever seen a Ventriloquist make a success of a 30 minute spot without a doll, well that was our dear Neville.

Another story....
When working in summer season at the Embassy Theatre in Skegness for Duggie Chapman, my sister brought her daughters baby in for a moment to show me. Her daughter had friends nearby and they were to spend the day with them whilst my sister saw the mattinee` show. The baby left but all the way through the interval I could hear a baby crying backstage – I left my tea going cold and spent the whole of the interval searching backstage – but nothing!

Then I caught Neville outside my dressing room throwing his voice and making baby sounds! (He said, "Caroline, you fall for it every time!")

Neville appeared in The Good Old Days many, many times

STEVE HEWLETT

Eastbourne, East Sussex

I first had the pleasure of working the *City Varieties* in 2004 in a ventriloquist based play for the Henry Moore Institute. It was my first introduction to this wonderful building steeped in show-business history. A stage that I know has opened doors to many of the great ventriloquists before me.

I have always enjoyed returning to this delightful theatre and in 2013, I made my 4th appearance there in *The Good Old Days* show with the wonderful Roy Hudd. The audience is always a welcoming one. They are there because they not only want to relive their variety days but to watch up and coming variety acts who are aiming to keep this genre alive. I have worked the *City Varieties* before and after the refurbishment and am pleased to say it has not lost any of its magic.

The artist book backstage was a delight to add my name to and I was thrilled to have signed the original book bearing the name of Charlie Chaplin. To follow in the footsteps of these wonderful entertainers makes me feel so humble. It is proof that variety is still alive and bottling those cherished memories when audiences return year after year. I was proud to reach the final of the 2013 *Britain's Got Talent Show* (coming 4th), which was an introduction to ventriloquism for a whole new generation - which can only be a good thing for variety. Long live Variety at the *City Varieties.*

JULIA BURNETT

Dartford

As a child, I well remember the delight I felt whilst watching famous ventriloquial acts on television and theatre shows. One of these names was the late and great Ray Allen and Lord Charles. I was totally mesmerised. Imagine then, the sheer thrill when I got to work with him on tour and at the *City Varieties*. He was a gentleman and pure class. He would often tell me he was going to, "Take me away from all this and treat me to a week in Mablethorpe, flying from Cleethorpes aerodrome." All to the amusement of his lovely wife Jane.

Ventriloquists obviously had an impact on me, as I married one -Alan Simmons. It was he who wrote a monologue for me about the *City Varieties* which I performed there. This went into the Archives at the theatre of which I am very proud. I was also lucky to play there with Danny La Rue and Sir Norman Wisdom and, on these occasions I used to enjoy (with dear Clarice) a cup of hot chocolate from the drinks machine in the green room. I later discovered that the water for this came from a tank in the loft and not from the mains! (I'm still here!) Nowadays, one of the acts I perform is a tribute to Hylda Baker and my husband is my Cynthia (he has lovely legs). Apparently, when Hylda played the *City Varieties*, she went to the bar and asked for champagne. When told they didn't have any she said, "I'll have a Guinness instead!" Priceless stuff for a priceless piece of our heritage.

JOHNNIE CASSON
Brighouse

The most magical theatre to work in. To me the *City Varieties* is full of 'Ghosts' - ghosts of all those who went before us. My first gig there went very well until I exited stage right instead of left and, as there was nowhere to go but to look at the brick wall, I did just that and had to stand there for twenty minutes. I didn't make that same mistake again.

I've loved working with many great artistes there. My favourite memory is of working the box routine with Jim Casey and Eli Woods. I played the Roy Castle part. It was magical and the audience loved it. Not only loved it but knew it. I could feel that they knew the whole routine and were actually anticipating every move.

Priceless memories in a Priceless Theatre

THE GREAT DESMONDO & CHERRY
Rustington, West Sussex

The *City Varieties* was the first theatre I ever played. It was 1967, I was 22 years old and had only been in the business professionally for a couple of years. The top of the bill was always the stripper and the rest of the show was a traditional Variety bill. The shows had wonderful titles like 'Strip, Strip Hooray' and 'My Bare Lady'.

It was a tough gig as the audience had really come to see the stripper and were mostly men and lads from Leeds University who were very boisterous. The lads from the University would sit in the boxes at the side and skim pennies down into the orchestra pit to try to shoot them through the skin of the snare drum. When this happened the musical director Johnny Rocket would stop playing. He would then stand up and tell them that if they didn't desist he would stop the show.

You did a band call Monday morning and the first show was a matinee that afternoon. It was the toughest show of the week as the audience had come to check out the new stripper - they certainly weren't interested in the supporting acts.

As this was my first theatre I had no idea that theatre stages had a rake and the *City Varieties*

has a very steep rake. My props were on a small table that had casters on so I could push it about. The stage manager Wally Coe said, "You'll open in number ones, while we strike the previous act, and you can set your props". Unfortunately, when the curtains opened, the draft was enough to set my prop table rolling down that rake and careering towards the orchestra pit. I saw this happening and was so terrified I was frozen to the spot and did nothing to stop it.

The table hit the footlights and tipped into the pit. Everything I knew was on that table. My whole act was gone. I was mortified. The audience, however, thought it was hysterical and screamed with laughter. The comic that week was Colin Crompton (later of 'Wheel Tappers and Shunters' fame). He was in his dressing room, heard the laughter and came rushing into the wings to see who was getting laughs on a Monday matinee. Michael and Stanley Joseph were in their office downstairs, heard the laughter and came up as they too had never heard laughter on a Monday matinee before.

I had no more material, everything was on the table so I went to walk off only to be met by Wally in the wings who said, "You're down for 12 minutes son, we're not ready for the next act yet." So, I had to turn and go back on stage, which re-doubled the laughter. The more discomfort I suffered the more they liked it. After what seemed like a lifetime later but was probably only two minutes, I looked into the wings, Wally said OK and I went off to great applause having done nothing.

In between houses I took the wheels off my table so that it could never happen again. For the rest of that week the act went perfectly with no more mishaps, which meant I died on my feet just like everyone else!

I went back to the *City Varieties* many times and always enjoyed the week in spite of everything. Years later I returned to do two pantomimes for Terry Cantor, both which ran until Easter - those were the days. I was delighted on a recent visit to do *The Good Old Days* to see the theatre is still thriving and going strong. The refurbishment backstage and front of house are excellent with the stage, the auditorium and circle bar remaining original, if somewhat cleaner.

I was also thrilled to find the finale photos of the two pantomimes I did were still hanging in the circle bar.

The Great Desmondo and Cherry

PETER (MACHINE-GUN) WALLIS 1926 - 2008

Rawdon, Leeds

City Varieties regular, Leeds own Comedian Peter Wallis was a 'big kid' at heart and when our grandson Rio was tiny, Peter and his wife Dot (She always signs herself with a dot •) would always be invited to Rio's Birthday Parties.

They usually bought him some toy or other but I dont know who enjoyed playing with them most, Rio or Peter. One year they brought him a bubble set and it was Peter who blew all the bubbles, "Have you a metal coat hanger?" he asked our Daughter Nina, after becoming bored with the usual small bubble maker given with the set. After twisting and bending it for ten minutes (with his hands, feet and teeth!) he'd fashioned it into the biggest giant bubble maker I'd ever seen. He stayed outside most of the afternoon blowing the biggest bubbles imaginable. Every time we looked through a window a huge bubble floated past!

Another year Peter bought a train set. This was no ordinary train set but one with authentic sounds of a train. Peter set it up in the garden and after every sound from the train he would mimic it. He got Rio to do the same. Then they began chug, chug, chugging around the garden in single file - like a train - a sight to behold. Peter on his knees ("Ruining his trousers," is what Dot said!) with Rio stood on Peter's legs. I don't know what the neighbours thought, but 4 year old Rio was loving it!

Peter was renowned for his quick-fire style of joke telling and was nicknamed 'machine-gun' as a result. He became a well-loved favourite at the *City Varieties* and appeared regularly on *The Good Old Days*

He joined Michael and Stanley Josephs Casting Agency - 'ATS Casting' based in Headingley, Leeds. They took him seriously and he was offered straight acting roles, which he loved. His acting career was quite productive and he appeared as many different characters in 'Coronation Street'. The last being Hayley Croppers 'Great Uncle Bert' where he spoke the immortal words, "Get your trousers on Harold and come home!" He appeared in dozens of TV programmes and big feature films including, 'Heartbeat', 'Open All Hours', 'Brassed Off', 'All Creatures Great and Small' and, my personal favourite, the role of a Priest in a wonderful 'Dracula' film alongside Bradford born Comedian Joe Belcher, Teddy Turner who hailed from Horsforth and Ted Carroll who had the *Hyde Park Hotel* in Headingley, Leeds. Also in this 1979 film was Frank Langella, Laurence Olivier and Donald Pleasence.

Peter trained as a fitness instructor before joining the army to train the troops. Because of his quick wit and funny temperament, they persuaded him to take up a professional career on leaving the army and he joined his family at 'The Peacock Hotel' in Rawdon which they ran. Two of his sisters were singers, the third was a pianist and his brother played guitar and also sang. Peter played drums and was a natural comedian. Later, Peter bought his own Hotel, 'The Westbourne' in Otley, Yorkshire, where together they made up a wonderful group playing to packed houses there with their comedy and variety show-band.

He was a very active man always doing something – entertaining, acting, playing practical jokes, thinking up costumes for his gags, trawling through charity shops for props (He loved hats and ties), spending time with his wife Dot, his Daughter Mitzi and Son in law Brian and his two grandchildren Jenny and Matthew (Who are both musically trained) A kind, warm and genuinely funny man he died on the 23rd May, 2008 and is still missed today. He was a good friend and colleague who loved life and was proud to be a Leeds 'Loiner' but, he was even prouder to announce...."I've been asked to play the *City Varieties* again!" - Ed

WARD ALLEN
Durham

I'm proud to say I've appeared many times at the wonderful *City Varieties* in the last 46 years. My first visit was actually my first full weeks work outside the North East after I turned professional. Opening on Monday 10th July, 1967, the show starred the musical family group, The Kenways. I had one spot in the second half, billed just above the exotic dancer! Top ticket price - 6 shillings (30 pence today).

We've had the pleasure of sharing the stage with many well-known artistes from the lovely and funny Dora Bryan to the shy and retiring Frank Carson. Our most recent visit was in 2006 where Roger and I followed Gordon and Bunny Jay doing their 'cod' vent act. I hope we showed them how it should be done! But probably the most unusual of our appearances there was an early morning visit for a wonderful variety show to welcome Father Christmas to Leeds. After the performance the acts paraded down from the stage into the auditorium and followed Santa out of the theatre and across to 'Allders' department store with the audience behind us. The theatre was always beautiful even if conditions in those days left something to be desired. The dressing rooms were very cramped, particularly if you happened to be sharing the room with a Scottish multi-instrumentalist who needed to tune his bagpipes. That was my cue to take Roger walkies! It was always a pleasure to work the *City Varieties*, receiving such a warm welcome from Peter Sandeman and his wonderful staff. I hope this unique and special theatre goes on forever.

CHARLES KNIGHTON
Cincinnati, Ohio, USA

In East London, there was an 83 year old singer of Ragtime Songs. That was Ida Barr who said, "Many a beautiful tune has been played on a fiddle as old as me." That was at Daniel Farson's Waterman's Arms hostelry.

I came over from The States in the 1960's to see the Blackpool illuminations which I had heard so much about. Whilst there, I heard what Barney Colehan was doing in Leeds, and decided to take a look. I have been over many times since (at least once a year, usually in the fall) and have never been disappointed. I usually manage to coincide a trip to the *City Varieties* Music Hall for *The Good Old Days* weekend with The Derby & Nottingham Association Luncheon who not only put on a splendid Sunday lunch, but supply entertainment as good as one would find in a theater. At my beloved *City Varieties*, a team of Chairman - Johnny Dennis warmly greets the audience; David Smith, Director of the band supports the artistes and Peter Sandeman, gifted past General Manager, adroitly mixed old favorites with new talent which, altogether produced a fresh *Good Old Days*.

I first saw Anita Harris supporting Harry Secombe in 'London Laughs' at the *Palladium* in 1966 and then later at the *City Varieties*. She recalled that she was a great niece of Ida Barr. I was amazed as it was that very same lady from London.

Leeds born Deborah McAndrews told us that, as a young boy, her grandfather and his chums would parody the popular song, 'The Boy In The Gallery' by singing, 'I love The Boy What Eats Mucky Celery' - That was one of my favorite songs but now, I can't hear it without thinking of those lines!

No comment on the *City Varieties* would be complete without mentioning the volunteer helpers who I have come to know very well. Their assistance is appreciated and I thank each and every one for their help in the past and, of course, for the future.

A life member of
'The Friends' of the City Varieties

MARILYN HILL SMITH
Cheltenham

Leeds *City Varieties* has long been a harbinger of happy memories for me. I was lucky enough to perform in one of the last televised *Good Old Days* with the legendary Leonard Sachs, produced by Barney Colehan. Most of the audience were dressed in period costume and looked wonderful. There was a long waiting list for a chance to attend one of these historic performances which made it more special for public and artistes alike.

In those days, backstage was very cramped but how the place has altered. It is now as good backstage as front of house!

I wish the *City Varieties* continued success in the decades to come.

PETE LINDUP
Blackpool

The first time I visited the *City Varieties* was when I was 6. My Grandfather, a drummer in the *Dewsbury Empire* orchestra would sometimes ' dep' for the regular percussionist there. Mum would lead me round to the stage-door where Grandfather would sneak me in to watch a matinee. I was too young to understand the jokes or why the ladies never seemed to have the time to finish dressing!

The next time I visited the *City Varieties* was part of Nuts and Bolts - a crazy musical act. Barney Colehan gave us a 10 minute spot in one of his *Good Old Days shows*. Not the TV version but a twice-nightly performance on four consecutive Saturdays. Having worked out our routine to last exactly 10 minutes we took to the stage but, not allowing for laughs, over ran.

Mr Colehan was not best pleased and ordered us to cut the act by a minute before the second house. We duly complied. The problem was when we got on stage we couldn't remember what we had cut, so the act was a bit of a shambles. We limped off to half-hearted applause only to be congratulated by Barney for running the designated time. He was obviously watching the clock and not us!

That was my last appearance with Nuts and Bolts before devising my own multi-instrumental act, which I've performed at the *City Varieties* many times. The audiences are always ' up for it', dressing in period costume, which adds to the atmosphere greatly. The recent renovations are spectacular, totally transforming the backstage area as well as the Swan Street area.

The *City Varieties* is a great venue with a unique as well as impressive history.

Long may it last.

Pete Lindup - Relaxing!

JIMMY CRICKET
Rochdale

When I was a teenager growing up in Belfast, I was totally captivated by *The Good Old Days* television series. Having aspirations to tread the boards myself, I was drawn to most variety shows on telly, but this one was special. The audience in their Victorian garb were as much a part of the show as the performers and their contagious enjoyment seemed to radiate into our living room. I remember comedian and fellow country man Frank Carson dancing on. He was the first Northern Ireland comedian to make it 'big' in the UK and his appearance on *The Good Old Days* was greeted warmly by our family.

Forty years on, I can still recall his first joke - "I've just seen a fella at the bus stop eating fish and chips and crying." I asked him, "What's the matter?" He said, "SOB, SOB, I've just crashed my new car, I've been declared bankrupt and my wife's leaving me. I'm going to throw myself under the next bus that pulls up." I said, "What are you eating fish and chips for?" He said, "You'd starve to death waiting for a bus around here!" - Dah Dah!

For the next five minutes he had the audience in fits of laughter, which he followed with two verses of, "Granny has left you her old arm chair," before jigging off to rip-roaring applause. That was it about *The Good Old Days*. Every act came out smelling of roses. The atmosphere made it that way.

When I got a break in a TV talent show called 'Search for a Star,' in the early 80's, I wrote to Barney Colehan - the brains behind *The Good Old Days* to see if he could catch me on the programme and hopefully book me for the show. To my utter delight he used me on his Christmas edition and, it was an even bigger break for me than the talent show. Barney even suggested my stage costume which has become my trade mark.

The TV show *The Good Old Days* and the *City Varieties* went together (and, still do) like cheese and onion or ham and pineapple. Forever etched in our memory when we think of the golden years of television variety. I congratulate the *City Varieties* on it's grand re-furbishment and it's many Anniversaries this year and wish it well for the future.

BERYL JOHNSON

Blackpool

The first time I played the *City Varieties* was in the late 1970's on a Duggie Chapman variety show starring David Whitfield, the Elsdon Twins, Jimmy and Brian Patton and full supporting cast.

What I recall mostly about the visit was the Stage Manager Wally Coe. He sat backstage all the time with a scruffy dog at his side.

I remember being in trouble with him when I received a phone call backstage. The phone was situated outside number one dressing room and I had been on a call for about five minutes, when Wally shouted, "I only allow anybody 3 minutes on the phone, there's other people waiting to use it and other calls coming in." I looked round. There was no-one even near me! For some reason, he really hated people using the phone and shouted at everyone when they did.

There was a jar of coffee and some tea bags on a table back stage and a big kettle. You could have tea or coffee, which he would make you for three pence. I remember he had a sweet jar to hold the money that he took.

What a character and the sort of Stage Manager who has now disappeared and you wouldn't find around today. There was also a lovely large blonde-haired older lady who worked in the front box office in the daytime. She was always very kind to the artistes and, in the evening she worked in the Circle bar. I believe she had worked for Stanley and Michael for many years and was really one of their key workers.

Walking on stage for the first time was a huge thrill for me, knowing that thousands of famous stars had played there. All their photographs were in the Circle bar - a wonderful collection going back a hundred years.

The year was around 2000 when, under the management and direction of Peter Sandeman, I played on a Music Hall Show. It starred Keith Harris and Orville and a great comedy vocal duo from the Midlands - Al and Dave Sealy with the stage name Cosmotheka. Sadly Al passed away during that same year but Dave continues today as a solo performer on Music Hall and Variety Shows.

I remember well meeting Stanley and Michael Joseph, they were real gentlemen of the theatre and treated their artistes and patrons alike - with great respect.

Long live the Varieties for future generations.

CLAIRE POOLE

Crossgates, Leeds

In 1959, I took my ten year old daughter, to a *Good Old Days* show to see Morecambe and Wise and Cardew Robinson. She had just bought herself a little autograph book and wanted to meet them all. So we hung around outside the stage door for ages but with no luck and, eventually had to set off for our bus.

Imagine our surprise when they passed us on the way to The Queens Hotel, where they were staying. Seeing the *City Varieties* programme in our hand they stopped to sign it for us. They chatted for a few minutes before Cardew, a real gentlemen, kissed my daughters hand. She was so thrilled.

LAWRENCE BELLHOUSE

Horsforth, Leeds

As a young boy in the early thirties, we resided at our business premises on Park Lane, adjacent to the Fire Brigade Headquarters in Park Street. One of our customers was a Laurie Hutchinson, the fire chief's son. Laurie had lost a leg in a motorcycle accident and though he still rode a motor bike he couldn't continue as a fireman. But, he managed to get a post as a Fireman Attendant at the *City Varieties* and, through this association we got lots of passes to attend shows there.

Most Saturday nights would find me in the queue waiting in the Headrow for the 1st house to exit, with a similar situation in Swan Street at the rear of the theatre. The queues were entertained by various 'buskers' - one, a paper-tearer was quite talented and, producing a newspaper from his raincoat he'd fold it in a particular manner before deftly tear off bits, seemingly at random from the wad of paper. Which, when unfolded became a wonderful lace tablecloth. The proverbial cap would be passed along the queue hoping for a few coppers.

We mostly sat in the front stalls and the advertising screen would eventually roll up to disappear in the uppermost area of the stage. How it rolled up puzzled me for a long time - but a line rolled around the ends of the pole in opposite directions was it's secret. The coloured beam of light emitting from the spotlights made visible by the smoke laden atmosphere of the auditorium was another source of fascination for me.

On the odd occasion we were seated in the upper circle where, as a seven year old, I would enjoy sitting alongside the spotlights watching the operator changing the coloured filters and adjusting the carbon rods to improve the produced ' Ark' to maintain the brightest light. This was the highlight of my visit along with the complimentary tub of ice cream that seemed to appear like magic at most visits. After the show, we would be handed a ' pass' for next week's show, often given to us by fireman Laurie. Ah, the *Good Old Days*. So aptly named.

Lawrence opened Nash's Tudor Fish Restaurant in Merrion Street, Leeds in 1963 where it became a rendezvous for artistes playing at the Grand Theatre and the City Varieties. Barney Colehan would go some Sundays for a grilled Halibut steak. After 40 years Lawrence handed it over to his son, Peter. - Ed

TONY ADAMS

Seaway

I first appeared at Leeds *City Varieties* in 2000, and for me it had the same feeling as walking on stage at the *London Palladium*. You are so very aware of all the great artistes who have appeared there before you.

The theatre epitomizes the essence of Music Hall. The dedication and enthusiasm of all the staff and volunteers, lead at the time by Peter Sandeman, made it a very special place to work.

It is a venue I shall never forget.

'Seaway' is a boat - Ed

DUO DU SOL
Frank & Jan Terry, Derby

We can't remember our first date at the *City Varieties* but Jan remembers being a dancer there in the 1960's. However, what we do remember is that we always had a great time there, especially when everyone would get together and have tea in the green room area in the interval and between shows. The audiences are special - so warm and responsive and we got to work with some great acts such as Frank Carson, Ruth Madoc, Danny La Rue, Bernie Clifton and many more. We usually appear on the *Good Old Days* shows.

The 'get-in' is always a performance in itself, as the driving and parking restrictions in the area were obviously devised by someone with a strange sense of humour to say the least. It is awkward to get one's car up Swan Street to unload and even worse to reload! However, it is all worth it when we get into the theatre. The backstage staff are wonderful. They really look after you and make you feel welcome. We remember it as it was with the old dressing rooms and, as basic as they were, they had a certain rustic charm about them. It made us feel quite nostalgic for the great days of Music Hall that are now such an important part of history. One thing that will never change is the rake on the stage - we performed an acrobatic adagio act from 1974 until 1990 and from

Calvero

1985 we also performed a comedy acrobatic mime act as Charlie Chaplin and The Rag Doll. We had to be so careful not to end up in the orchestra pit! The *City Varieties* is now a beautifully refurbished building and will be able to carry on in far into the future. Long may it continue.

PETER JOHN
London

In 1959, right at the start of my career I played Father Bear in 'Goldilocks' at *The Grand Theatre* and, during rehearsals, I went with the company on my first visit to the *City Varieties* to see their seasonal offering - 'Babes In The Nude'. No, not a panto, but a rather saucy show featuring comics and strippers, all rather naughty and highly enjoyable!

The local theatre chaplin told us later that he once found the bill-topper at the Varieties in tears as the snake she used in her her act had gone into winter hibernation and was not as 'perky' as usual. "Of course," said the reverend gentleman, "I could not provide her with another snake, but I gave her what comfort I could."

I first met Barney only after the TV series had sadly finished in 1983 but after that, I worked regularly with him in Music Hall at the theatre, during which time Wally, the ancient stage-doorman was a familiar fixture, sitting immobile with his grubby dog in his old, Green Room armchair.

I have been happily engaged almost every season since (plus two Panto's) and the *City Varieties* remains my top favourite venue. Long may the great tradition of Music Hall continue there!

STEVE CLARK
of The Clark Brothers

Steve, one half of the wonderful dancing duo, The Clark Brothers who appeared many times on the TV version of *The Good Old Days*, says,
"I wish The Friends of the City Varieties another successful 25 years".

Brinsworth House, Twickenham, Middlesex
Brinsworth House is a retirement home for artistes founded by The Artistes Benevolent Fund

MAUREEN WOODHOUSE
Beeston, Leeds

Once, many years ago, when I was walking down the Headrow in Leeds this man walked quickly by me and almost tripped me up. He turned around and I saw it was Clinton Ford of 'The Old Bazaar' in Cairo fame. He apologised and explained he was in a hurry to get to the City Varieties.

I laughed and said that I was going there too later that day. He asked my name and during his performance, he gave me mention. I was thrilled.

JACK GREENWOOD
Rawdon, Leeds

I well remember as a lad going to the City Varieties. Me and my mates were working in a mill in Bradford. Once a week, as soon as the whistle blew, we'd be off and onto a bus heading for the City Varieties.

We loved the variety ' turns' and we also bought a drink. We only had the money for one drink each but felt so grown up in the bar. If my Mum had found out she'd have gone mad. But, looking older than the 16 we all were, we got away with it and went for years. Happy days!

FRANCES INGRAM
Garforth, Leeds

My first visit to the City Varieties was in 1973, when I was a member of Kippax Amateur Dramatic Society and we were fortunate to obtain tickets for a televised Good Old Days show. We had seats in the stalls so had to come in costume. I remember having to learn the words to the songs before the show started and those of us who wore modern-day glasses had to remove them, therefore some of our group had difficulty seeing the show.

My next visit, was to a stage show around 1990. Soon after this I joined 'The Friends' of the City Varieties and, a few years later became a front of house volunteer. About ten years ago I joined 'The Friends' committee and I have been secretary for the past 7 years. I have been fortunate over the past few years to be present at the last show prior to the re-furbishment in 2009 and the opening show in 2011.

It was a great honour for me to meet Her Majesty The Queen and The Duke Of Edinburgh when they officially opened the re-furbished theatre on 19th July, 2012. They were very interested in 'The Friends' and the work they do and wished the theatre every success.

Frances is Secretary of ' The Friends'
Executive Committee

ALAN J VAUSE
Pontefract

As a schoolboy I was in a few choirs and Mum said I had a nice voice so when Carol Levis came to the City Varieties one Saturday with his Carol Levis Young Discoveries, I auditioned. I sang two songs - 'Star Of God' by Eric Coates and 'Christopher Robin'. There were hundreds of people auditioning and I couldn't believe it when I got through.

I was sent off to London (my mother as chaperone) for training and was assigned a singing tutor. Thoroughly enjoying my time and making good progress, the war came along and spoilt it. Buildings were being bombed every day and so, to keep us safe, Carol Levis suggested we all left for home. Back in Pontefract, I finished school and began a life in showbusiness.

I found an agent, Johnny Pellar, joined Equity and became a semi-pro with a day job and entertained in the evenings and at week-ends.

I appeared at the City Varieties many times and always felt as if ' I'd come home' as that was where I'd started my long career. After a few years, I became a full-time professional artiste and toured extensively but always enjoyed being back in Yorkshire. At Batley Variety Club, I worked alongside many great artistes - Trini Lopez of If I had a Hammer fame, Marti Caine, Duggie Brown, Bobby Knutt and many, many more. At 83, I've had a wonderful life - all due to the City Varieties.

RONNIE RONALDE
Ipswich

When I was part of 'Steffani and his 21 Silver Songsters' and we had completed our Monday morning band call, the conductor, because he had a new drummer, decided to run through the National Anthem. What we didn't know was that the music of 'God Save The King', normally played at the end of the show - was the cue for the rats to appear, eating all the food strewn all over the floor by the audience during the performance. The rats came out in their hundreds. Well, we couldn't move fast enough. We fell over each other on stage and in the pit. It was not rehearsed again!

The next time I appeared there, there was not enough room to accommodate us all on stage in one line, so the last few boys did their act in the dressing room!

MALCOLM DURNAN
Liverpool - Aged 91

I went with my parents for years to see the pantomime. It was the best one in Leeds and we all loved it. Then I took my children and then my grandchildren. They now take their kids!

RIO FRANCISCO SUAREZ
Holmfirth, Yorkshire
Aged 11

My first experience of the *City Varieties* Music Hall Theatre was in 2006 when I was four. I was introduced to pantomime by my Grandma who you will know as Caroline Fields. I have been on my annual trip there ever since.

We like to share a box so we can really get into the spirit of things. I have a perfect view and can feel the action on stage. In the interval I always look forward to having an ice-cream and try not to let it drop over the edge because it once did - they were still wrapped. (Well, actually the one I dropped was Caroline's!)

I love the feel of the *City Varieties*. It is welcoming and friendly and has a great family atmosphere. As soon as I walk in through the door I feel the excitement of what's to come. I also feel at home as if I am amongst friends. I always look forward to the pantomime and get really involved. The actors used to throw rocks (actually they were sponges) but now they throw huge soft balls. All the children and most of the adults collect them and throw them back...it's brilliant fun.

PHIL COOL
Chipping, Lancashire

Well folks, I've just done my last gig as I've retired this year. (I know, no more pulling funny faces). However, I didn't want you to think that I'm not thinking of you! I've loved performing all these years and one theatre which stands out in my memory is the *City Varieties*. (Apart from *The Palladium*!) I've loved entertaining there. The audiences are always fabulous. The theatre so special. Keep it safe. Love from Phil.

MALCOLM POVAH
Bolton

I first appeared at the theatre in 1992 and recall the trepidation and misplaced apprehension arriving for my first rehearsal. Such feelings were soon allayed as I was made to feel most welcome by Johnny Dennis and the staff who spent no time at all in ushering me backstage to meet Clarice - the 'concierge' and hospitality host 'par excellence' who promptly brewed up for me before we got down to business.

"These people have their priorities right," I thought. "What better than a cup of Yorkshire tea before band call." I was billeted high up in a garret dressing room, top of the house. "Oh, you're up in the angel suite," laughed one of the stage hands when I asked for directions to my dressing room. I remember climbing the almost perpendicular flights, overloaded with suit bags, banjo and my treasured straw hat, wondering if John Buchan had worked the theatre prior to writing his '39 steps!' As I rounded the first landing my heart sank as I was confronted by another flight of stairs. The treads of this flight were likewise worn shallow by the endless access and egress over many years of theatrical traffic.

Finally, I burst exhausted into my shared attic condominium and fell into a heap on the nearest chair. It was there, after moments of quiet repose, that I became aware of a 'coo', 'coo', 'coo,' that seemed to be going on all around me. "I don't know about Angels," I thought. "More like a bloody pigeon cote!" Just then, approaching footsteps entered the room. It was Phillippe - the international illusionist and dressing room cohort. "I've just come to feed my birds," he said. "If I don't do it now, they be dropping the white stuff all over the stage later on". Yes, what I thought were pigeons were in fact, Phillippe's beautiful white doves! Silly me - Coo. Coo. Coo!

Malcolm Povah

BERNIE CLIFTON
Derbyshire

I began my career as a teenage vocalist in a dance band in my home town of St. Helens and then 'progressed' to pubs and clubs. Whilst I was singing, I was also learning to play the trombone which must come naturally to me as I've been asked to play all over the world - "As far away from here as possible," is what folk actually say! I've played the trombone at the Beijing Olympics and again, in Las Vegas, as a member of the Pukka Pies English Band. Well, someone spotted me and, in the 1970's, I found myself working on the BBC TV series, 'Crackerjack' with Michael Aspel, Peter Glaze, Don Maclean and Jan Hunt.

However, I still hadn't really started to use props on stage which I enjoyed doing until, in October 1971, I was appearing on *The Good Old Days* with Les Dawson, when I told Barney Colehan that I couldn't be as funny as Les. Barney said, "Don't try to be. You're a visual comic. Follow your heart and perform the way you want to, not the way of other comics." Many years later Barney said to me, "See, I didn't put you wrong, did I?" Barney and I became firm friends and I've appeared many times on the televised version of *The Good Old Days* and on the stage version too. Every time I appear at the *City Varieties*, I feel as if I am coming home. The audiences really are the best. We always have a great time together. It has a truly magical feel, a small intimate theatre with a big sense of grandeur.

DUGGIE CHAPMAN MBE
Blackpool

2d, get ice-creams for us in the interval at 3d a tub and, at the end of the show we would head round the corner to a cafe which sold Pie and Peas for 5d. In the cafe, which was opposite the stage door of the *Victoria Theatre* or the VIC as it was known locally, many of the acts would call in after the show. I remember them all eating pie and peas in their Crombie coats and hats, still in full make-up. No wonder I was stage struck at such an early age.

On leaving school I joined 'The Four Blue Pages' run by a gentleman called Harry Leslie, a semi-retired entertainer and Dame comedian. In the group was another young man named Bobby Breen who later became the wonderful star Larry Grayson.

We toured the length of the British Isles on variety shows each year. I was the longest serving member of 'The Four Blue Pages' and, over the years, had many new page-boy outfits which was our dress.

Aged 18, my voice turned into an unmusical croak overnight, so I had to leave the group. (Bobby Breen had left much earlier.)

I decided to turn to comedy having written down hundreds of gags I'd heard over the years from the comedians we worked with and, using the best ones, got myself a week at 'Collins Music Hall' on Islington Green. This was an old music hall with an enormous history and I remember how tatty it was, however this was a mecca for agents and show-bookers.

My new act went well, and during the week, I was approached by an agent called Don Ross - married to Music Hall star Gertie Gitana - who

On leaving school in Burnley at the age of 15, I went straight into showbusiness. I had been taken to the *Victoria Theatre* and the *Palace Theatre* in Burnley every Monday from the age of 11 by my Grandmother, who loved the variety theatre. She would say, "Come on, get ready. We're going to see the TURNS tonight." I was hooked.

It was a regular Monday visit to the first house where she would buy a programme for was running a stage circus and a memories show of old stars called 'Thanks For The Memory'. Don booked many theatres throughout the country and managed many acts.

He asked if I would like to join a show in two weeks time called, 'Piccadilly To Paree', I was delighted.

We rehearsed in London in a dingy rehearsal room In Gerrard Street, Soho, then went on the road. The man running the show was Tommy Seymour and our first date was the *City Varieties* in Leeds.

The revue ran for about two years - and we toured every theatre there was - yes, there were variety theatre's in every town and I loved it.

I remember the digs where I stayed on that first visit to Leeds. It was run by one man and called, 'Novello House,' simply because, and we must have been told this twenty times, Ivor Novello stayed there whilst playing Leeds in one of his well-known musicals. He even showed us the bed Ivor slept in.

After the week in Leeds, I played the *City Varieties* many more times in 1961 and 1964 and, when I went into business as a producer, I often played my own shows there for Michael and Stanley Joseph.

Great days and great memories. Long may it reign for many more years to come. Keep supporting this great venue.

THE FAMOUS **CITY VARIETIES** · 6-15 · MONDAY 9th NOV. 1964 · 8-15
LEEDS   Telephone 30808   MATINEES TUESDAY AND SATURDAY at 2-30 p.m.

PEEPARAMA

KENNY CANTOR
THAT GREAT COMEDIAN

★

JIMMY SCOTT

FROM THE NITE SPOTS OF THE WORLD

LORRAINE BURNETT
THE STRIPSTAR

THE GAYBELLES

DUGGIE CHAPMAN ★ **VERONICA DEAN**
PETER BRENT ★ **BRIAN RAMSEY**

Printed by Electric Gladney Printing Co. Ltd. Manchester 3.

Above: "Peeparama" with a young Duggie Chapman in support   Below: Duggie in "French Sauce"

THE FAMOUS **CITY VARIETIES** — LEEDS
Telephone – 30808   Telephone – 30808

6-15 + **MONDAY, DECEMBER 4th, 1961** + 8-15
MATINEES TUESDAY & SATURDAY AT 2-30 P.M.

BY POPULAR DEMAND ! !
THE RETURN OF THE MOST EXCITING STRIP STAR OF THE CENTURY

FERNANDA CANOVA

IN

"FRENCH SAUCE"

with

REGGIE   **CANDY**   **ALEC**   **DUGGIE**
DENNIS   **MAYE**   **HALLS**   **CHAPMAN**
THE FAMOUS COMPERE   SUGAR AND SPICE   A CAVALCADE OF JUNK   THE COMEDY PERSONALITY

+   BILL DANE AND HIS REVUE BALLET   +

BOBBY KNUTT
Sheffield

I was always sad that I never appeared on the TV series *The Good Old Days*. It was 150% pure showbiz and in the finest Music Hall venue on planet earth. The first time I worked there was in a spring season of Peter Sandeman's *The Good Old Days*.

The back-stage area in those days was cramped and, whilst it was never grubby, it was definitely well worn. I was topping the bill so I got number one dressing room (nearest the stage). I closed the door and sat for a wee while, trying to think of the show-biz legends who had passed before me and felt very humble indeed. Flanagan & Allen, Ted Ray, Tommy Trinder, Max Miller, Tommy Cooper, Morecambe & Wise and Tessie O'Shea to name a few.

I've worked there many times since and one thing that always cheers me immensely - the staff never change. The back-stage lads are always there as are David Smith and his band and Charles the technical wizard. One lady I did miss last time, when I was there in April 2013, was Clarice. Clarice seemed to live in the small back room next to the number one dressing room - it was actually the 'green room'. She was tea-lady and biscuit baker, button sewer-onner, zip mender, tie tidier and, anything you needed to know, you asked Clarice. She also took the kitty for the tea, coffee and biscuits. Mmm...those biscuits!

I remember one season I did there when I was topping the bill, Clinton Ford was there but below me in billing. I felt embarrassed that this wonderful entertainer who had topped the charts on so many occasions was on before me. I used to sing his songs when I first started

with my group, stuff like 'Fanlight Fanny' and other funny ditties. He was, and still is, one of my heroes. His dressing room was on the top floor up two flights of hard concrete stairs so I asked him if he would like to share my dressing room. He was overwhelmed. We shared wonderful memories that week-end. Having said all this, my favourite reason for working *The Good Old Days* is sharing time with Mr Johnny Dennis, the finest chairman in the business. He sets the audience up so beautifully that, by the time I go on at the end, it's impossible to fail. It is a unique venue and has a special place in my heart. Long may it reign.

SHEILA MATHEWS
Southwick, West Sussex

When you walked out on stage the audience looked like a flower garden with their fancy costumes and hats. The array of colours and textures hit you like the audience of no other theatre. It was a sight to behold - breath-taking! Everytime I appeared at the *City Varieties* the welcome was enormous. The first time I came up to Leeds was for the Pantomime 'Cinderella' where I played Prince Charming. Sheila Burnett was 'Cinderella'. The Ugly Sisters were Brian Blade and Johnny Heawood.

You may think that this pantomime ran for the Christmas season. No such luck. We actually performed it for the *Good Old Days* so had to learn a whole script for just the one recording.

We all had costumes made to measure too and had to learn new songs as well as the script. A whole version for just one night!

Last time I appeared was with Danny La Rue where I did a tribute to Jessie Matthews. Dear Barney Colehan titled it, 'Mathews does Matthews'.

Barney was a wonderful man and very kind and patience. That was providing you got everything right. Happy Days.

GEOFFREY BRAWN
Brighton, East Sussex

As Musical Director for the Players Theatre I would take rehearsals and write out all the vocal arrangements. It began as a six week engagement which turned into 40 years. Artistes liked my style and so the likes of Dora Bryan and Beryl Reid would ask me to play for them.

In the 1960's for the BBC, I was on a show called, 'Before The Fringe' which involved topical material. They needed a pianist and I would play 2 or 3 numbers on every show.

I've accompanied artistes like Danny La Rue, Barry Cryer, Bernard Cribbins, John Inman, Georgia Brown and Tessie O'Shea. They would all rehearse with me in Villiers Street at Charring Cross before going up to perform at the *City Varieties* Theatre.

I also accompanied young singers and dancers who performed the opening routines for *The Good Old Days* shows. The show gave a lot of artistes their first experience of theatre, some of whom went on to greater things. Many Congratulations to 'The Friends' of the theatre.

GEOFFREY GOSLING
Roundhay, Leeds

My first visit to the *City Varieties* was on Wednesday 19th October, 1960 for a recording of *The Good Old Days* for the BBC. I still have my ticket, I was sitting on Row L in the stalls. For this occasion, I had travelled from the Calder Valley by bus in full Edwardian costume, complete with a straw boater. I can still remember getting some very strange looks from the other passengers. No matter, I was sixteen, and looked forward with great expectation to the performance ahead.

I finally arrived at the theatre to find, to my astonishment, the seating area in the stalls had been partially removed to accommodate the cameras and technical equipment. But, even so, that evening was a wonderful experience which I shall never forget. Since that evening I have been to the *City Varieties* many times, seen many musical stars, many in their latter years, and have always come back for more. It is very gratifying to see this lovely old theatre restored so sympathetically to it's former glory. Long may it be cherished by the citizens of Leeds and beyond.

Geoffrey has appeared many times at the City Varieties - Ed

CYNTHIA AND LEON ROVER
Gildersome, Leeds

On one particular visit to the Varieties, Ken Dodd was on the bill. We had booked a table at a restaurant for after the show but when Ken began his performance by asking the audience if everyone had brought their flasks and sarnies, we realised that any hope of having dinner that night was very unlikely!

SIR RICHARD STILGOE

Surrey

If you are a solo performer, touring around the country doing one-man shows, variety is a big treat. You get to be part of a company and to meet your heroes.

I did three stints on *The Good Old Days* and, as a result worked with Les Dawson, Roy Hudd, Roy Castle and many other great performers. I also got to do material I had known since I was a boy – from old books of music hall songs my Mum owned and Stanley Holloway records the family owned. So, I got to sing 'The Night I appeared as Macbeth' and recite 'Three ha-pence for a foot' which Marriott Edgar wrote for Stanley Holloway and was, I think, on the B-side of my 'Albert and the Lion' record.

I was also allowed to write a song called *The Good Old Days* and sing it with the orchestra conducted by Bernard Herman (not to be confused with the American Bernard Herrman who wrote the terrifying music for Psycho).

Another thing I remember is the surprise on walking into the theatre and finding only one side of it beautiful. I don't know whether the money ran out or what, but only the stage-left side of the auditorium had been restored – which you didn't notice on television, because Barney shot it cleverly – leaving the other side (the one the audience at home never saw) a sad relic of rougher times.

The audiences costumes also stuck in the mind – fabulous attire all provided by the audience themselves. Another surprise was that every week a large party of Swedish enthusiasts came to Leeds to be in the audience. We never understood why, though this was before Abba so perhaps they didn't have much choice back home.

One lovely memory I have is of Peter Skellern and I playing there when a large party of WI members were in the audience. Peter and I had written a surprise song for them called 'The WI Calendar' – all about Jam and 'Jerusalem' – and setting the scene nicely for them to sell their Calendars and Christmas Cards.

I always had a wonderful time there. It is a unique theatre and I send everyone my best wishes for it's endless future.

Sir Richard is noted for his songwriting and his clever wordplay and wrote the lyrics to Andrew Lloyd Webber's Musicals, 'Starlight Express', 'Cats' and 'Phantom of the Opera' - Ed

ANDREW VAN BUREN & FAMILY

Fred, Connie, Andrew and Alyson, Newcastle-Under-Lyme

Our family's history with Leeds *City Varieties* spans 53 years. My parents Fred Van Buren and Connie Greta originally performed there as the Amazing Yoxanis presenting their magic and illusions act.

Their first appearance was in 1960 as the speciality part of the night-time show, ' Light Up The Town'. The matinee show at the time was Harry Corbett and Sooty with Harry Cody & Doris as their supporting act. At the time, the Amazing Yoxanis manager, Don Ross was the sole booker of the *City Varieties* for the Josephs so, quite often, if they had a gap in the diary Don would put The Yoxanis in, which created regular appearances for a number of years. The Yoxanis first television appearance was on *The Good Old Days* on the 18th

October, 1961, and televised live in black and white. Gladys Morgan, Joan & Frank Laurie, The Amazing Yoxanis, The Gaunt Brothers, Barbara Law, Ken Wilson and Chairman Leonard Sachs were also on the bill. As always, the Producer was Barney Colehan and the Musical Director was Bernard Herrman.

Then, exactly 50 years later, I appeared there in *The Good Old Days* stage show during the opening season after its major refurbishment. It was both strange and wonderful to think that my parents had stood on the same spot 50 years earlier.

Agent Pauline Marks, who shared an office with Don Ross, decided it was time to change The Yoxanis name to get them onto the number one theatre circuit and so, from 1962, Dutch illusionists Van Buren and Greta were launched. It was the same Yoxanis act just redressed and with a Dutch accent.

This worked, opening new doors for them in London and around the world. They also worked for Walt Disney. So, there was a gap of *City Varieties* appearances for them from then on.

When Stanley and Michael Joseph re-launched the stage productions of *The Good Old Days* in the 80's they re-booked my parents. Then later, I appeared with my juggling, plate spinning and magic act. That was the beginning of my numerous appearances there for the Joseph Brothers and then Peter Sandeman.

We've loved every appearance on that famously beautiful, but very raked, stage appearing with some wonderful acts - Barry Cryer, Nuts and Bolts, Geoffrey Durham, Tony Adams, Ami MacDonald and, of course, Chairman Johnny Dennis who we had the pleasure of touring with on a number of occasions in the Danny La Rue Show.

It remains a theatrical bookmark and one of the few places where you can see true variety acts. We all wish it a long and happy future.

NICHOLAS PARSONS OBE
Buckinghamshire

The *City Varieties* is a very special Music Hall with great history and tradition. Nearly everyone of note has worked there some time or other, and I had the pleasure of doing my comedy routine in a Music Hall bill on more than one occasion for Peter Sandeman. The audiences are most warm and receptive. You have the feeling that they think that this is their theatre and want to make you feel special.

There was one hilarious occasion when we were recording two editions of 'Just a Minute' there. On arrival, our Producer informed us that one of the panelists he had engaged was, at the last minute, unable to make it. 'Just a Minute' is a show where you cannot just slot anyone in, it has to be someone who has some experience of playing the game. It was too late to get someone to fly up from London, so he had the inspiration to contact Charles Collingwood, who appears in 'The Archers' and had played the game a few times. 'The Archers' is recorded in Birmingham and Charles said he would finish at a certain time and drive straight to Leeds.

He hoped to be there before the recording began. Time was ticking away, and still no Charles. Paul Merton had the inspiration to say, "Let's start the show as if he is here and improvise accordingly. After all, it is radio and his physical presence is not vital." It was a gamble whether he would arrive in time to join us.

As you may be aware, the stage door of the theatre has now disappeared and you make your entrance through the auditorium. We were playing the game with an imaginary Charles and I was making such remarks as, "Charles has yet to score." "In fact, he hasn't contributed much yet." All of which, the audience loved.

We had been going for about 10 minutes when suddenly, there was a disturbance at the back of the auditorium and in strode Charles.

He got an immediate round of applause and I had to explain the situation to the listeners. Charles took his place on the panel as if he had been there from the start. The whole procedure was a gamble which paid off magnificently but, in professional terms, we were living dangerously and my improvisational skills were truly challenged.

MAX MILLER 1894-1963
Brighton
"Now Here's A Funny Thing"

Mention the name of Max Miller to any comedy fan and chances are they will remember, or will have heard of, 'The Cheeky Chappie' as he was known. Thomas Henry Sargent was born in Brighton on 21st November, 1894 and was to rise from the humblest of beginnings to become the most famous stand-up comedian of his generation and Britain's highest paid variety star.

Max's career has been well documented, from his earliest experiences of entertainment in WW1 concert parties, Jack Sheppard's Entertainers on Brighton seafront, touring revues and cine-variety.

His wife Kathleen, who he married in 1921, is credited with coming up with the name 'Max Miller' and the outrageous stage costume for which he would become famous.

Throughout the 1920's Max continued to learn his trade and in May 1929, George Black put him on a bill at the *Palladium* for the first time. Max was heard on radio in 1931, including Radio Luxembourg. But, frequent brushes with the BBC over his 'blue & white books' sometimes restricted his appearances.

The following year, 1932 saw Max release his first 78rpm record, 'Confessions of a Cheeky Chappie'. That was the start of a 30 year recording career where fortunately, he had the foresight to record his live performances on several occasions and these can still be heard today.

In 1933 Max made his big screen debut in 'The Good Companions' and this was the start of a nine-year film career including several starring roles. Max played all the great variety theatres and appeared in three Royal Variety Shows in 1931, 1937 and 1950. During WW2 he entertained Londoners during the 'blitz' in revues including 'Apple Sauce' and 'Haw Haw'. Max briefly flirted with TV during the 1950's but he much preferred a 'live' audience to a TV camera.

On May 7th, 1963 Max died at his Burlington Street, Brighton home, where there is now a blue plaque.

The Max Miller Appreciation Society was formed on 29th January, 1999 in Brighton and since that time it's many notable achievements to its credit include the erection of a life-size bronze statue, the erection of two blue plaques on properties owned by Max, the naming of the Max Miller walk on Brighton seafront and an exhibition of photo's, posters, programmes etc., in a local fish restaurant.

It also publishes a quarterly magazine, 'There'll Never Be Another', has regular bi-monthly meetings, holds a charity Garden Party every August and a convention weekend each November.

The Society has also assembled an important collection of Max memorabilia. MMAS also has a website www.maxmiller.org where details of membership can be found.

JOSEPHINE DOUGLAS
Wakefield

As a keen member of the Leeds Girls' Choir (aka over many years, the Elizabethan Singers, the Yeldarb Singers, Melismata and now Upper Harmony), I visited the *City Varieties* in support of two of our various celebrity vice-presidents - the Gaunt Brothers. They presented a super selection of their topical and satirical songs but, I found myself hugely embarrassed as a young girl, to find that there were nudes appearing in the same show! Cue strong blushes until that part of the show was over.

Among the amazingly diverse range of presentations which have been staged at the *City Varieties*, from pantomimes and pop performances to top comics and musicals, taking in along the way of course the unforgettable *Good Old Days*. One event which stands out in my memory is taking part in a huge charity concert during the 1990's and being crammed, along with a large number of fellow Choir members, into a much-too-small dressing room up several flights of steps - but we loved every minute of it.

As a member of the audience, I have enjoyed several brilliant Flaming Charity shows (the Fireman's charity), which mixed professional and amateur performances to great effect. But one of my favourite memories is of seeing Richard Stilgoe and Peter Skellern weave their musical magic in a presentation which included the first stage performance of 'The W.I. Song' in front of Women's Institute members who sparked off the wonderful 'Calendar Girls' and who were there to sell the very first W.I calendar. Some time later - with special permission from Richard Stilgoe - a fellow Choir member and I were delighted to be allowed to perform 'The W.I. Song' for some of our own audiences.

More recent visits to the City Varieties include seeing a superb edition of *The Good Old Days*, headlining Bernie Clifton and featuring Caroline Fields - herself an ex-member of the Leeds Girls' Choir, as we are proud to tell people - and last year, a backstage tour of the theatre with the Choirs' long-time Dortmund partner group, the Florian Singers, who were thrilled to explore the building, hear some of its fascinating history and actually be allowed to sing on the stage.

More power to the Friends' metaphorical elbow. Here's to the next 25 years!

ANTHEA HARDACRE
Ilkley, Yorkshire

We had tickets for a television recording of *The Good Old Days* and had hired costumes from Homburgs Costumiers. We left the children with our neighbour saying, "We should be back around 10.30pm. See you then." She said, "Don't worry, I've plenty of sewing to get on with. There's too much for one night," she laughed. "You'll have to go out again tomorrow!"

At the *City Varieties* we were told that, due an industrial strike, the show would go ahead but would not be televised. The great comedian Ken Dodd was on. When we arrived home at 1.30am our neighbour was fast asleep on the sofa - the sewing all done!

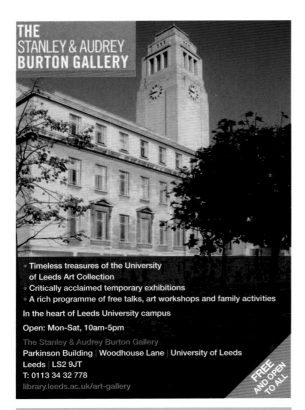

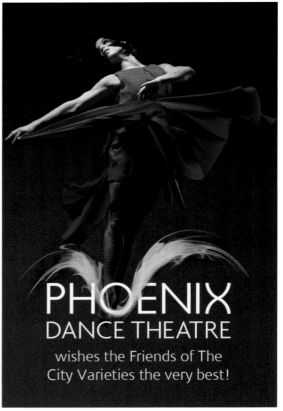

lots of love & good wishes to the "friends of The City Varieties Music Hall" g love wonderful Happy memories

Barbara Windsor x

Over 50 years of appearances at the City Varieties!
Still going strong - Keeping Variety alive.

Best wishes from The Van Buren Family

www.vanburen.org.uk

Deryck Thorp
Honorary Life Member of the
Friends of the City Varieties

would like to wish the
Friends of the City Varieties
a long and
successful future.

It has been a pleasure
working with and meeting
all the artistes and other
Friends serving on the
Executive Committee.

Gail Sandeman

would like to wish
The Friends of the
City Varieties
a very happy
25th
Anniversary

and continued
success

THE MANAGERS BOOKS

Overleaf are four extracts from 'The Manager's Books' in the year 1897 - the salary column is in code.

(11) - the 15th day of March - The 8, Lancashire Boys. Charlie Chaplin was in this group as young lad. Walter Munro was a dancer and he topped the bill. In the 'remarks' section, the Manager has written 'worth' the 'W' he paid. The 'Sisters Laurie' were 'poor' and 'Hal Croueche' was 'bad'. There should have been ten acts on the bill that week but, Agnes Hazel 'did not appear'.

(16) - the 19th day of April (Easter Monday) - Vesta Tilley was on the bill and the Manager has written that she was 'good' whilst Steve Mc Carthy was 'bad'. On this bill, of the ten acts booked, four failed to turn up. It looks like Marie Kendall, a comedienne was paid what looks like £16/-/- (£16 pounds) for the weeks engagement.

(34) - the 23rd day of August - Lily Langtry was on the bill. 'The Crosmans' were 'good at £6.0.0'. and Harty, a Conjurer was 'good' and 'worth £9.0.0'. Whilst it says he was worth that amount, we are not told whether he was paid thatl

(44) - the 1st day of November - G. H. Elliott On the bill (which is in poor condition) for the 1st day of January, 1900, there are comments for the speciality act, 'The Brautfords', which says, 'not worth the money.' And, for 'Queenie Alluro' - she was 'alright at this price.'

Engagements for MONDAY, the 15th day of March 1894.

ARTISTE	Business.	Salary.	Agent.	Position on Bill.	Remarks.
The Highleys	Musical Act	C W	B & A	Large	Good. Work T
Agnes Hazel	Seriocomedienne	F	O & H.		Did not appear
Griffin & Dubois	Comedians	O E	O & H.	Bottom	Good
Sisters Laurie	Duettists	E	Self		Poor
{ Hal Crousele	{ Description Vocalist	T	F. Y.		Bad
{ Flora Gaunt	{ Male Impersonator				Good
W. Dew	Baritone	W	Self	Large	Good
Walter Munroe	C & Dancer	O U	Self	Top	Good Work G O
8 Lancashire Boys	Clog Dancers	T	Self	Large	Good
Lulu Gould	Serio	O U			Good

Charlie Chaplin was in this group

Easter Monday.

Engagements for MONDAY, the 19th day of April 1894.

ARTISTE	Business.	Salary.	Agent	Position on Bill.	Remarks.
Marie Kendall	Comedienne	C W 16/-/-	Foster	Bottom	Good
Bishop & Ricardo	Specialités	I	Self	Large	Good
Steve McCarthy	Comedian	B	Foster		Bad
Harriet Vernon	Burlesque	U	Self		Did not appear
Miss Martin	Serio	A	Self		Did not appear
Master Sherwin	Ballad Vocalist	A	Self		Did not appear
Devereaux	Dogs	T	Pacey	Large	Good
G. Newbarn	Comedian & Mimic	W	Napoli		Did not appear
Nano Hono & Hana 2 turns	Ring Act & Trapeze	G C			Good
Vesta Tilley		C U U			Good
G. Bastow	Comedian	E U			Good

Marie Kendall

Vesta Tilley

Engagements for MONDAY, the 28th day of August 1897

ARTISTE	Business.	Salary.	Agent	Position on Bill.	Remarks.
Lily Langtry		X	Hamor		
Effie Desartelle		X	Hamor		
Jean Stanley		X	Lacey		
Frank Leon		X	Self		
Lizzie Kirk		X	O. & H.		
Sullivan & Sullivan	Irish Sketch	X	Clanton		
Wal Grae	Descriptive	B U	Self		Good
The Cosmani	Duettists	B U	Self	Lge	Good @ £6.0.0
Little Tim	Comedian	T	Slay	Lge	Good
Hardy	Conjurer	G E	Slay	Bottom	Good worth £9.0.0
Bransby Williams	Mimic	C O	Foster	Lge	Good
Benson & Vaite	Duettists	W	Self		Good
J. W. Rowley		O E	Self	Top	Good
		£ T U U			

Lily Langtry.

Engagements for MONDAY, the 1st day of November 1897

ARTISTE	Business.	Salary.	Agent	Position on Bill.	Remarks.
Dan Crawley	Comedian		Foster		Good
Lilian Bishop	Serio & Dancer	G O			Good
Peggy Pryde	Comedienne	O E	Self	Top	Good
Lewin & Lewin	Patter Vocalists & Dancers	W	Claxton		
Bob Vokes	Comedian	G O	O. & H.	Lge	Good
Nell Geraldine		W	Higham	Lge	Did not appear
Alec Hurley		D O O U	Higham	Top	Good
Geo. H. Elliott		D			Good
Bros. Alexander	On chief				Good
Otto & Hylton		E			Good

G. H. Elliott

Telegrams :

"BILLIBOB,"
WESTCENT, LONDON

Telephones :

OFFICE
TEMPLE BAR 8891-9270
PRIVATE
ELSTREE 1069
✦✦✦✦✦✦✦✦✦✦✦✦✦✦✦✦

DON ROSS

AGENCY

SUITE 25,
140a,
SHAFTESBURY
AVENUE,
LONDON,
W.C.2.
✦✦✦✦✦✦✦✦✦✦✦✦✦✦✦✦

This Agency is not responsible for any non-fulfilment of contracts by Proprietors, Managers or Artistes.

This Contract is subject to the conditions of the Music Hall Arbitrator's Award 1919.

EMERGENCY CONTRACT

An Agreement made the....24th....day of....December....19 51

between....British Union Varieties Ltd.,....hereinafter called the Management of the one part, and....Billy Moore....hereinafter called the Artiste of the other part, **Witnesseth** that the Management hereby engages the Artiste, and the Artiste accepts an engagement to appear as....Accordianist & Yodeller....(or in his usual entertainment) at the Theatres, and from the dates for the periods and at the salaries stated in the Schedule hereto.

SCHEDULE

The Artiste agrees to appear at....12....Evening performances per week at a salary of £ 13. 10. 0

....2....Matinee £ : :

Total £13 : 10 : 0

....1....Week at City Varieties, Leeds....commencing Jan. 21st....19 52

....Days Rehearsal at....11 a.m.

....Week at....commencing....19

....Days Rehearsal at

....Week at....commencing....19

....Days Rehearsal at

....Week at....commencing....19

....Days Rehearsal at

Bill matter, etc, to be sent to....Harry Joseph Esq.,....to arrive at

City Varieties, Leeds....not later than twenty-one days before opening.

Signature.................................

Address ....

The Croydon Press, 889, Romford Road, E.14.

*One of Billy's contracts for the City Varieties
21st January. 1952 for 12 evening shows and 2 matinees*

BILLY MOORE
Langney Point, Eastbourne

I first had the pleasure of working at the *City Varieties* in January, 1952 where there was always a nude act on the bill. That particular week they had the Chinese Kee Sisters, billed as 'The World's only Chinese Nudes'. I remember that they did not have sinks in the dressing rooms but a washbowl on a stand and, after the show, we were provided with a very large jug of hot water.

We had to have band-parts for the 12 musicians in the pit orchestra and I would try to get to the theatre early on Monday morning to be first to place my band-parts on the stage. This was to get an early band-call in case other artistes on the bill might want to perform any of my numbers. (Band parts were very expensive to have written out so I didn't have many other songs to select from).

Digs in those days were from £2.10 shillings to £4.00 a week which included a hot meal when you got in after the show and use of the cruet!

Billy Moore - taken on stage at the City Varieties in 1952

My second booking there was nine years later on 4th September, 1961 when the show was called, 'Strip, Strip Hooray' and, by that time they had wash-basins with hot and cold running water. The pit orchestra was now reduced to four musicians and my fee had increased from £13.10 shillings to £25.00 a week - by then, I was playing the piano accordion which I bought in Nuremberg, Germany in 1956 when playing in cabaret there. My third booking there was in August, 1962 with no increase in fees. George Lacy was top of the bill. He kindly let me share his dressing room near the stage for the week as he felt sorry for me having to drag my piano accordion up the stairs to my dressing room - at the very top of the house - up two flights of narrow, well-worn stone steps!

I am now 87, active and in good health, but gave up working two years ago as the piano accordion gets heavier as one gets older but, if there happens to be a piano nearby or on holiday then I'll give it a whirl.

In the 1950's these are some of the digs I stayed in.

Mrs. Furman, 75, Cowper Street, Chapeltown Road, Leeds 7. I paid £4 for the week, which was well above the average, but it was close to town so I could walk to the theatre. It was very comfortable and she served good and plentiful Jewish food.

Mrs. Senior, 143, Meanwood Road, Leeds 7. It was £2.10 shillings a week. This was recommended by Pauline and Ricardo. It was excellent with good food and lodgings. This was the cheapest and always busy so I had to book early. (By letter - no phone back then other than public)

Mrs. Lazenby, 290 Cross Flatts Grove, Dewsbury Road, Leeds. I paid £3.10 shillings a week. Recommended by Locky and Henry. It was comfortable, the food was good, but it was a long walk to the theatre.

Yorkshire Evening News. Tuesday August 28th, 1962

City Varieties

George Lacy, who has appeared many times in Yorkshire pantomimes, returns to Leeds this week in his usual loveable role - the buxom brassy dame.

A girl with a continental flavour, Delina, has top-billing with her strip act in this entertainment-packed revue 'Evening in Paris'.

Opening the show on a breezy note are Brenda Oliver's Six Follies Girls who are followed by cheery radio entertainer Ray Peters, who introduces the artistes.

Magic with a strong flavour of mirth are the ingredients offered by Chris King and Joyce and Billy Moore is well received with his yodelling and accordion playing.

Photograph of the City Varieties old entrance on The Headrow

KEITH HARRIS
Blackpool

I was first asked to do a week at the *City Varieties* Theatre in Leeds in the sixties. I think I was offered £75 for the week - matinees and all. I was to do a spot and compere the show between the 'nudes'. The thing was - I looked so young and had to wear short pants to stay looking young as my billing was 'Keith Harris the Boy Ventriloquist' - the other artistes 'mothered' me!

In 1973, I was booked to appear on *The Good Old Days*. I had watched the show so many times and loved every one so, for me, it was a great honour to appear there. However, it was the first time Orville had been seen on television and, more importantly, it was the first time I had ever worked with him, so it was quite a risk. At the time, I was appearing in 'The Black and White Minstrel Show' at *The Hippodrome Theatre* in Bristol for the Christmas Season. Orville arrived on the Saturday and the Television show at the *City Varieties* was on the Sunday. Although I had designed him, at first sight I was not sure about his look so, after I had put a voice to him, I took him into the dancers dressing room at *The Hippodrome* to see what they thought. They loved him. So far so good.

Then, off I went to the *City Varieties* with Orville. That night, for the first time ever, I walked out on stage with the duck on my arm and, as he turned around from my shoulder, all the audience gave a great big ahhhh....and then I knew he was going to be a big hit. We appeared four times on the televised version of *The Good Old Days* where Orville first made his debut. It was the best time ever.

ROGER HOLMES
Manchester

I was first introduced to the *City Varieties* in 1953 when the late James Towler and I had a spat in 'The Performer' about the relative merits of the Varieties and the *Barnsley Royal*, both having been recently redecorated. We met, agreed to call a truce and became firm friends, making many theatre visits together (James subsequently became the Yorkshire correspondent for The Stage' newspaper).

Co-incidentally 1953 was the year that Barney Colehan launched the long running series *The Good Old Days'* from Leeds.

In those days one went in by The Headrow entrance to be greeted at the head of the stairs by 'Pip' Pawson, one of the 'old school' managers, in his smart dinner suit. Somewhere about would usually be Stanley and Michael Joseph, with the boss man, Harry Joseph often there at the back of the circle with his oxygen cylinder.

The circle bar was something special, with it's wonderful array of photographs, and you never knew what notables you might find in there. The entertainment fare then was often a revue with some posing involved and a title like: 'The Naughty Nighties' or 'Strip, Strip, Hooray' from producers such as Richard & Hicks, Harry Dennis & Dick Ray, Terry (Toby Jug) Cantor or Jack Gillam. Paul Raymond brought 'The Jane Show' and other salacious offerings.

The pit band was not very good, to put it mildly, getting down to just four members latterly. For 'Harry Joseph's Big Show' in 1958, it was augmented and had Stanley Clarke-Brown (late of the *Halifax Palace*) as Musical Director. Donald Peers, Jimmy James & Co and Ted Lune were headliners in the programme with some strong supporting acts, though what those good folk who came to see Donald Peers thought of the Exotic Sheila, who came on a bit strong, is not recorded. She even frightened me! A theatre in competition with the organisation and resources behind the *Leeds Empire*, just around the corner, had to carve it's own niche. The Varieties did, helped no doubt by the television exposure. *The Empire* is long gone, its rival soldiers on. It's a very different world now, but some of us over 80 can cherish our memories.

*Journalist, Speaker and Founding Member
and Chairman of the
Manchester Music Hall Association*

WILL SHEPHERD
Manchester

*Remembering my Dad - Howard Shepherd
of Sheps Banjo Boys*

Dad used to work a lot in the Manchester area where there were many theatres at the time. Whilst working in Manchester, he was spotted and offered work at the *City Varieties*. He said 'Yes' but worried how to get there. Dad didn't have a car (hardly anyone did in 1930) so used to travel on public transport - dressed in his evening suit and carrying his banjo case and his 'dots' under his arm. I know he appeared more than once at the *City Varieties* which was for a week at a time. As well as his stage work, Dad used to broadcast with the BBC playing banjo and later, the piano accordion. He worked with lots of great artistes, amongst them Wilfred Pickles, Donald Peers and Arthur Worsley. (Photo taken in 1935)

IAN CLAYTON
Bradford

I was taken on a junior school trip to the *City Varieties* to see a pantomime which would have been in the late sixties, before I left George Street junior mixed school in the summer of 1970 - when The Kinks were singing about 'Lola' and Mungo Jerry were ' Stretching right up to reach the sky'.

My only memory of the pantomime is of the Dame slinging an egg, or pretending to sling an egg, over the heads of the audience. In my adolescent mind I thought that must be what people did in theatres, sling eggs! I knew even then though that the *City Varieties* was a special place where the spirits of the performers of long ago still floated like peeling paintwork or smudged greasepaint.

When I did telly programmes, I did a few from this magical place where I recorded during the day and then stayed behind to watch the show. I laughed more than I had ever laughed when I saw the late great Norman Collier tread the boards there. He did his broken microphone routine and even though I knew almost every line off by heart I still laughed just at the thought of what was coming next.

Another time, a man called Harry Fisher presented me with a piece of wood from the old stage. I still treasure that splinter. It lives in a little bag on a shelf in my office.

For Yorkshire Television, I filmed many series of a programme called, 'My Yorkshire' and when we filmed Caroline Fields for her programme within the series, I filmed her from there whilst she was appearing in a *Good Old Days* show. Some of the crew hadn't been there before and were spellbound by the sheer history of the theatre and the array of talent on stage that night.

Five years ago, I actually got the chance to perform from this ancient stage myself as my friends in 'Chumbawamba' were doing a show alongside a comedy magic act and asked me to compere. In my fantasy I thought I would compere from Leonard Sach's famous box and I bought myself a wooden gavel and prepared a lot of big words. Sadly the box wasn't there that day, but I right enjoyed myself anyroad and I still tell folk that I once chaired a show there. I've recently been teaching in Changcgun University in China and one of the things that seems to fascinate them are my tales of Yorkshire and our culture. Amongst others, I show them photo's of the *City Varieties* which they love to see and hear about - I even try to sing one or two of the old songs you might hear there. As you can imagine they scream with laughter when I try to do a cockney version of, 'My old man says follow the van' or 'Boiled beef and carrots'.

"Sing to us again," they say, "Just like you would on stage." At least I can get away with it over there!

Leeds *City Varieties* is a treasure box full of history and has a lid that can't be closed, so stuffed full of gems it is.

I once interviewed Ken Dodd about the importance of theatre's to towns. He said, "Think of every focal point that a town has and put them all together and that is the theatre". I don't think I can say better than that.

VERA & BOB CAREY
Alwoodley Lane, Leeds

One day, many, many years ago whilst on a day's shopping trip to Leeds, there was the worst thunder storm we had ever seen. We were on a coach from Halifax for the day and, as it was summer, we had dressed lightly. Well, we wandered around aimlessly for hours getting wetter and wetter, had some lunch and then looked at each other. What to do until the coach left at 6.00pm?

We were sheltering in an arcade and looked across the street to see a sign saying, the *City Varieties*. The *City Varieties*? "Goodness, it must be twenty years since I was last there," said my husband Bob. Taking my hand, he dragged me as fast as he could across Briggate to the entrance of the theatre.

"Yes, there is a matinee show," we were told at the box office. "Finishes at 4.20 pm". Just time to get a drink in the bar too before the performance. Once in the Circle bar we felt at home. The whole theatre was so enveloping and warm with an ageless atmosphere we found we just didn't want to leave. And we didn't. We've now moved to Leeds and go back often.

MICKIE DRIVER
North London

My appearances at the *City Varieties* have given me many happy memories. I was thrilled to be part of a show I had watched on television since childhood and delighted to find it such a happy experience. Johnny Dennis makes everyone welcome - the audiences are always a joy - the theatre staff helpful - David Smith and the gentlemen in the pit are first class and the turns enjoy the green room as much as the show.

I've enjoyed working with everyone on *The Good Old Days* but remember the lovely Anita Harris, the irrepressible Bernie Clifton and the amazing Clark Brothers. I see Steve Clark (now in his late 80's) when I visit Brinsworth, and he can still tap along with the best of them. Long may the *City Varieties* continue to provide entertainment that entertains!

ANITA HARRIS
London

I have been playing the wonderful *City Varieties* for many years and it never ceases to entertain me! Maybe it's the Yorkshire folk who are warm and friendly and love to be entertained. Or, maybe it's because of the building itself - old, full of atmosphere and history. Whatever it is - it's special! I always look forward to my return visits there.

Mickey Driver and Anita Harris at The Good Old Days

VINCE HILL
Henley-on-Thames, Oxfordshire

When I first worked the *City Varieties* it was to appear on *The Good Old Days*, produced by Barney Colehan for the BBC - and, what a show it was too.

As I have travelled around the country through the years, many people have asked me, 'Why don't we see it on TV anymore'. I have to say, 'I don't know - ask the BBC!'

I have always been convinced that this show would get great viewing figures if it were brought back because it was an entertaining, well-produced, colourful and vibrant show. Thank you Barney - it had great appeal.

One thing I learnt very quickly at the *City Varieties* is there are no super stars or divas there. I had been driving for four hours to get there. Couldn't find it. Didn't know where to park and was feeling more than a little stressed. God, I thought, just let me get to my dressing room and have some peace and quiet and collect my thoughts. There at last with bags and suitcases, et al all sweaty and hot - I found my dressing room where I discovered I was sharing with another artiste.

So, no matter who you were - you were all in it together - No superstars - No Divas! But, when you are sharing with the likes of Ken Dodd, John Inman and Larry Grayson well you save your ego, stardom and talent for the stage.

I look back on those days and think about the happy times... funny times... at rehearsals... tired times when you're through with it all and having a glass or two in the bar after the show. But, then the comments... Good Show eh? Brilliant... Marvellous. And, the pleasure of having had the audience joining in with their sort of songs - and me delighted to hear them singing along to my hit successes, 'Roses of Picardy', 'La Vie En Rose' and 'Love Letters in the Sand'.

Then back to the hotel with the laughter and applause still ringing in your ears - Bed and then up the next morning and off again to God knows where.

I have been retired now for over a year, after 55 years in showbusiness, but will always remember with great affection the marvellous times we all had at the *City Varieties*.

Long may it continue.

DEREK GRANT

Dorset

As Producers, we have many happy memories of bringing shows to the *City Varieties*. One particular Saturday evening, about 10 years ago, we were touring 'The Bachelors' Show with John Stokes from the original line-up plus Jonathan Young and Kevin Neill making up the group. Our special guest was veteran comedienne and trumpet player Dottie Wayne - a very funny lady.

Whilst everything was being set up for the band-call, I went across the road to get some sustenance from McDonald's for my partner Michael Jones and myself. As soon as I stepped through the door I heard, "Whatever are you doing here?" and I turned around to find I was face to face with one of my young cousins who had just started at Leeds University. She explained that she and her boyfriend were in Leeds to go 'clubbing'. But, when I told her about our show they cancelled their plans and decided to come to a real variety show instead.

The Bachelors with John Stokes

We got complimentary tickets for them both and I watched as they sat transfixed, mesmerised, lapping it up and loving every minute. They were discovering what proper entertainment consists of. (And, incidentally, the rest of the audience were heard muttering, "Now, that's what I call a show," as they left) As for myself, when I think of the *City Varieties* I say, "Now that's what I call a Theatre".

DOREEN HERMITAGE

Essex

I first appeared at the *City Varieties* around 1964 as a professional trained solo dancer. I had many successes in the West End at the larger venues including, ' The Talk of the Town'. After joining the *Players Theatre* I started to choreograph there. At the same time I was dancing and choreographing wherever I was asked and spent three years at *The Royal Shakespeare Company*. One notable piece of theatre there was 'Much Ado About Nothing' alongside Derek Jacobi.

After I'd been at *The Players* for a few months, Leonard Sachs went to Barney Colehan and said, "You've got to have this girl." I appeared at the *City Varieties* many, many times in the BBC programme, *The Good Old Days*. I sang and danced to songs like, 'Flanagan, Flanagan, take me to the Isle of Man again' and, 'I was a good little girl til I met

you,' where I would tease Leonard Sachs. I would duet with different artistes too like Teddy Green and Jan Hunt.

Barney also asked me to back Roy Castle, Danny La Rue, Lorna Luft, Peggy Mount, John Inman, Anita Harris and Sheila Steafel where I would gather my dancers and choreograph a suitable routine. Danny loved us to be involved and called us his 'lovelies'. We wore beautiful costumes to compliment whatever the principal was wearing.

I also did a comedy striptease when Max Bygraves was singing there one time. How he kept a straight face I'll never know!

One of my strangest requests was to train professional football teams which I have done for many years and, if you want a laugh - apparently it's on something called 'You-tube!'

MARGARET GIBSON

Cookridge, Leeds - Aged 90

Back in 1936 there was almost NO *City Varieties* as I remember one of the dancers setting fire to the curtains. It was whilst I was a young trainee dancer at the *Imperial Training Academy* on Woodhouse Lane, near Leeds University, that our troupe was asked to take part in that year's pantomime.

We had a chaperone who we called 'Mother' and she luckily spotted the curtains smoldering - set on fire by one the older dancers - who was caught smoking in the wings during rehearsal. She was showing off to us younger girls. However, Mother made sure she didn't show off again. She got the biggest telling off in front of the whole cast and crew and never smoked again!

JOANNE MARTIN

Leeds

One December in the late sixties, my boyfriend Terry and I were sitting in the Piccadilly Bar. I knew that the pantomime showing at the *City Varieties* was 'Snow White and The Seven Dwarves', and also that there was an adjoining door from the theatre to the bar. Terry was unaware of either of these facts.

We had had a few drinks and it was obviously the pantomime interval, as down the stairs facing us came seven colourfully dressed small men in single file. I pretended not to notice, when Terry suddenly said, "Did you see that?" "See what?" I asked, to which he proceeded to explain what he thought he had just seen. I just looked at him with a very incredulous expression.

About ten minutes later, he said, "There they go again, didn't you see them this time?" "I think you have had enough, don't you?" was my response, but he went on to protest that he had again seen several small men walking across the bar and disappearing up the stairs. I carried on the pretence for a while, before I let the cat out of the bag and we had a good laugh.

ANNETTE (AND PETER) RILEY

North Farm Road, Gipton

I haven't been to the *City Varieties* for a while and would love to see another performance but have to be careful with the lights as I have epilepsy.

I remember when I was a little girl, I went with the NSPCC to see 'Cinderella'. What a fantastic performance it was. Then stewards came round with ice-cream and I asked if I had to pay. I didn't, but was told they were very cheap. I bet the ice-creams are more expensive now!

FRANK MURTON

Meanwood, Leeds - Aged 80
Married to Dorothy for 54 Years

When I was 18 I couldn't get in the *City Varieties* as I was 'baby faced' and looked only 14. I waited outside whilst my friends went inside to see the show 'Halt, Who Goes Bare'.

I did National Service and, home on leave, decided that finally I would try to get in to see a show at the *City Varieties*.

With my uniform on I looked much older and got in only to find that the famous Phyllis Dixie was appearing that night and it was standing room only. I was right at the back and couldn't see a thing!

JAN ODDY

Old Forge Mews, Bramhope, Leeds

It was about 1967/8 when my first husband Les Stones (who had MS) was sitting in his wheelchair in our sitting room watching *The Good Old Days* on TV which he never missed.

I had put the chip pan on (We did have one that long ago!) and had gone upstairs for a few minutes. Suddenly, I smelt smoke and rushed downstairs. I opened the kitchen door to see the chip pan on fire and the curtains well ablaze. Having dealt with it, I dashed to see if Les was alright. He was sitting there engulfed in smoke, still watching *The Good Old Days* and completely oblivious to it all.

HENRY IBBETSON
Brook Nook, Leeds 10

In the late forties as youths, we were regulars at the *City Varieties*. We would go and see Phyllis Dixie and Jane of The Daily Mirror who were thought to be a bit rude but by today's standards, were very tame indeed.

But, top of our list was that wonderful Irish tenor Josef Locke. It was well known he liked a drink so the time to go was the last performance on Saturday night where he would sing the rehearsed songs but did not finish there for he would continue singing.

Even the closing of the curtains didn't stop him as he would come through them. He had us all singing for another half hour until, eventually, the crew would flash the lights. And, if he didn't take any notice of the flashing lights, the crew would put the house lights on and the stage in blackout. Even so, he would always come back through the curtains again for one last bow when we would all stand and cheer!

Great times at our own wonderful *City Varieties*.

BRIAN HIGGINS
Leeds

In the 1960's I was a Police Officer at Millgarth Police Station, (the old one). When not busy I would sometimes 'sneak out' (as did many others) and ' sneak in' through the stage door of the *City Varieties*, standing in the wings to watch.

One evening I was talking to the 'wing man' - not the correct name but he was the one pulling the ropes for the curtains as the next act came on. As she passed, she gave me her dressing gown to hold and went on stage to do her act.

During her performance the 'wing man' said casually, "Your super (Superintendent) is in tonight," and pointed upwards above my head.

Looking up I saw the toes of a pair of shoes sticking out from a gantry about 12 inches above me. I hung the dressing gown on a convenient peg (actually a rusty nail) and left quietly.

As I turned to leave, the wing man whispered, "What? You're going to walk out on Phyllis Dixie?" and shook his head.

GLADYS BENN
Leeds - Aged 87 - The only one left out of nine children - My Mum

Entertaining my mum Gladys
with Sisters Denise (left) and Susan (middle) - Ed

When I was a young girl I used to go with my Mum to the *City Varieties* to see all the strip shows. She went once a week despite being, 'deficient in funds' as she called it. She said it was her only pleasure. (She also said that of the odd cigarette and a tipple of sherry!)

Of course, there wasn't just a stripper on the bill. It used to be a good strong variety show with dancers, singers, maybe a juggler and a comedian.

There were seven of us sisters all pleading to go with her, but it was the one who got to the only pair of silk stockings first who actually went.

SIR BRUCE FORSYTH CBE

Virginia Water, Surrey

I will always be very grateful to the *City Varieties* Music Hall Theatre. My first appearance there meant so much to me and it also helped me at a very difficult time. It is a very special theatre and holds many fond memories. I well remember the City of Leeds too. A vibrant, exciting place to be and the people were so very kind to me. My good wishes to the Friends and good luck in everything you do for this wonderful old theatre.

ANTHONY (TONY) CLIFT

Leeds
Talking about his Grandma
- Lucy Brennan

In the early 1940's I lived with my Grandma who had been a Music Hall Artiste. She was billed as the 'Original Lancashire Comedienne'. When she retired she kept a boarding house in Woodhouse where I came to live to avoid the bombing in Tyneside.

Various stage players stayed with her. Among them was Tod Slaughter starring in 'Sweeny Todd, the Demon Barber of Fleet Street'. For a treat I was taken to see the show and was shown around the back of the theatre.

I remember the general squalor and the musty smell of sweat and perfume which was an anti-climax as I imagined it would very grand. However, everyone was kind and I was given a good seat for the show.

When the Demon Barber said his famous line, "I'll soon polish you off," to the unfortunate customer having a shave, all the audience shuddered and groaned thinking how he would end up as a pork pie.

It is all so different now being a lovely refurbished theatre. What my Grandma would think of it now is anybody's guess. Happy Days.

CHRIS YOUHILL

Queenswood Heights, Leeds

In the early 60's I worked on the buses in Otley with a friend - I lived in Ilkley, he in Pool. Every other week we were on the early shift so, every alternate Tuesday, we always went to the City Varieties. They were grand shows with diverse acts on each bill.

Of course, this was in the days when celebrated lady strippers appeared, notably the very famous Phyllis Dixie who was a very attractive lady indeed.

How times have changed though. Her act and those of similar artistes were so tasteful and tame that if today's inquisitive and daring young bloods had seen them I doubt they'd have raised an eyebrow! Her signature tune was, of course, 'Is it true what they say about Dixie'.

The resident dance troupe did two or three spots every night and were pretty good. They were called 'Bill Dane's Revue Ballet'. There were four girls along with Bill Dane - a very dapper chap in black costume and a superb top-class dancer who attracted a lot of sarcastic whistles and dubious comments from certain ribald members of the audience, when male dancers were regarded as ' pansified'.

There were three girls of average height who all knew their routines well and one tall one who, frequently turned left instead of right and so forth. When the girls were in the middle of a fairly vigorous routine one evening, my favourite suddenly clasped the top of her strapless costume, fore and aft and quite destroyed the dignity of the performance by loudly proclaiming, "Oh, me ruddy zip's gone!" A true trouper, she managed to leave the stage, still dancing.

Considering the limited dimensions of the stage the girls always managed a very impressive Can Can - she of the embarrassing frock being the one to have the furthest cartwheel to achieve her stage exit - and the whooping and shrieking was commendable and would have been acceptable in the 'Follies Bergere!'

Those of us who have been fortunate enough to take part in Peter's guided tours of this wonderful old theatre have been especially lucky to stand on the stage where so many of the 'greats' entertain us. Our thanks are due to everyone at the City Varieties past and present, especially Peter Sandeman, for their tireless work on our behalf. I look forward to my next visit.

CONNIE POWELL

Chorlton-cum-Hardy, Manchester

My sister Barbara and I were lucky enough to be at the very first televised performance of The Good Old Days, broadcast by the BBC, in 1953. We have never forgotten our excitement at being there - it was magical and still is!

FREDA BUCKLEY
York

In the 1950's, I went many times to the *City Varieties* with my Sister Edith. We could only afford seats in the upper circle or even standing in the gods. But, because of the intimacy of the theatre, still felt part of the audience. We could see and hear clearly and saw wonderful shows.

Now we sit in the dress circle or even share a box and still see some wonderful shows. They have never lost their magic or perhaps its theatre itself!

BILLY BEDLAM
Shaw, Rochdale

Last time I was on the bill for The *Good Old Days* was April 2008. Topping the bill on this occasion was Roy Walker. Prior to the matinee show on the Saturday, Manager Peter Sandeman was touring the theatre with some guests. I had two hours before 'curtain up' and was interested in learning more about this wonderful theatre so I cheekily tagged on to Peter's guided tour. He was very knowledgeable and a great tour guide, telling us about the history of the theatre and about the plans for the refurbishment. We followed him up the rickety steps as he gathered us all centre stage to talk about the ornate plaster work.

"We have had a team of sculptors into the theatre of late. You see the lovely plaster stucco work here?" Peter asked, pointing to one of the boxes, "Well, they have taken rubber moulds from these wonderful old plaster carvings to make an exact replica. This will take the theatre back to its original Victorian state. Even the colour schemes will be original when the work is finished." At this point I looked up to the ceiling and noticed the lovely chestnut brown colour that ran the full length of the roof. I hadn't noticed it before because when you perform on stage you are blinded by the lights. Although I was intruding and eves-dropping on Peter's tour, I couldn't resist asking the question, "Peter, will they be keeping that lovely brown ceiling?" Peter laughed, "No, it will be replaced by a pastel pink." "That seems a shame," I said. "Not really," said Peter, laughing again, "That's nicotine. Some say it's over an inch thick in places." How times have changed.

INCORPORATING THE VARIETY ARTISTES FEDERATION

CONGRATULATIONS
TO THE FRIENDS OF THE LEEDS CITY VARIETIES
ON 60 YEARS
OF
THE GOOD OLD DAYS

FROM THE YORKSHIRE BRANCHES OF EQUITY

NORTH WEST YORKSHIRE VARIETY BRANCH
Branch Secretary: Valerie Jean Mann
Tel:0113 2853848   e-mail: val@mrstipsy.co.uk

SOUTH YORKSHIRE VARIETY BRANCH
Branch Secretary: Joy Palmer Tel:0114 2644833 e-mail:chuffinells@hotmail.com

HUMBERSIDE VARIETY BRANCH
Tel:01484 848031   e-mail: equityvbn4@msn.com

YORKSHIRE RIDINGS GENERAL BRANCH
Branch Secretary: Pete Keal Tel: 01422 855211 e-mail: equity.yrgb@gmail.com

AREA ORGANIZER: Nigel Jones NORTH EAST OFFTrF
Tel:0114 2759746   e-mail: northeastengland@equity.org.uk

CALLING ALL ENTERTAINERS !
JOIN EQUITY & LET EQUITY SUPPORT YOU

NORMAN COLLIER 1925 - 2013

Welton, East Yorkshire

We were at the 80th birthday party of comedian Peter Wallis. The evening was at an end and everyone had begun to leave. At around midnight, Norman went into the car-park behind the venue (Horsforth Rugby Club) to get his car. We stood talking to his wife Lucy just inside the doorway. He was gone ages and Lucy was getting agitated, "Where on earth he is?" she moaned, as all the other cars were driving out.

Norman Collier's Funeral: Bobby Knutt, A Man, Roy Hudd, Peter Sandeman, Freddie (Parrot Face) Davis, Johnnie Casson

I went to look for him and outside, in the pitch black car-park, I shouted for him. Suddenly, from out of the shadows came a car and stopped in front of me. It was Norman who then wound down the window and began his fighter pilot routine complete with goggles, helmet and gloves. I was crying with laughter and slowly, coming out to see what was going on came Peter and Gail Sandeman and John, my husband. Followed by Peter and Dot Wallis and finally Lucy.

Without speaking, Norman then got out of the car and went to the boot. Hidden from us he exchanged his fighter pilot gear for his balaclava (complete with yellow beak) and started his chicken routine.

By now the houses opposite (facing onto the car park) had twitching curtains and lights came on in upstairs windows. He went through routine after routine. All in the car-park with an audience of seven, "Why didn't you do all that inside?" asked Lucy, with folded arms.

"I would have done, but I wasn't asked," was Norman's frank reply.

Lucy just shook her head, "Never mind him. Just let him get on with it and get it out of his system. He's like a bloomin' big kid!" At that, he laid on the floor of the car-park with his arms and legs in the air and pretended to cry like a baby.

We were all bent double with laughter. Lucy went inside!

Wherever he went he played celebrity golf, raising thousands of pounds for charity and wherever he went, his love of horse racing would also prompt him to have a bet on the horses - sometimes even winning!

CITY
PALACE OF VARIETIES

Managing Director - HARRY JOSEPH   Director - STAN JOSEPH
Manager - "PIP" PAWSON

LIFE OF A
MUSIC HALL

PRODUCED BY KENNETH CARTER AND BARNEY COLEHAN

1. THE VARIETY GIRLS
2. MARIE LLOYD (JOAN TURNER) "Don't Dilly Dally"
3. HARRY CHAMPION (ARCHIE HARRADINE) "Any Old Iron"
4. FLORRIE FORDE (MARJORIE MANNERS) "Till We Meet Again"
5. HELDA AND LEE, "The 1920 Girls"
6. FE JOVER AND JACK, "Comedy Acrobats"
7. STAN STENNETT, Comedian
8. DORIAN CLAIRE AND VARIETY GIRLS
9. JOAN TURNER, Comedienne
10. GAUNT BROS. "Two Voices, One Piano"
11. ROBB WILTON, Comedian
12. DORIAN CLAIRE AND VARIETY GIRLS

Narrator : DERYCK GUYLER   Chairman : DON GEMMELL
Musical Director : ALYN AINSWORTH

WEDNESDAY, JANUARY 7th, 1953

96

STAN STENNETT MBE
Cardiff

I first played the *City Varieties* in 1953, alongside the great Rob Wilton. It was a great experience and, in showbusiness, everyone felt that they'd 'arrived' if they were booked to play that particular venue. I dressed up as a gentleman 'toff' to do my act and when you played the *City Varieties* you had to construct an act that was different from your normal one. No 'modern' jokes. Everything had to have a sort of 'period' feel about it and some of the acts on the bill even played as being great music hall stars of the past, such as Marie Lloyd and Harry Champion.

I loved the way the Master of Ceremonies gave his ' floral' and wonderfully long-winded

Stan in a sketch with Leslie Crowther at the City Varieties.

introductions to each performer, "At enormous expense," etc. I also loved the way the audience entered into the spirit of things and dressed up in Victorian and Edwardian dress. It really was fun on both sides of the footlights. We always had a full orchestra in the pit. I especially remember Alyn Ainsworth's Northern Dance Orchestra with the great Ken Frith on piano. Back there only a few years ago, very little had changed. It is, and remains, a gem of a place and I feel honoured to have been one of the artistes to have trodden its boards.

Stan at the City Varieties.

LIZ STANDERLINE

Moseley Wood Gardens, Cookridge, Leeds

This is one of the tickets I had for *The Good Old Days* on Sunday 20th December, 1981. Unfortunately, due to heavy snow all over Leeds we couldn't get there. It was such a shame as we had hired costumes for the event and were so looking forward to the show. But, it was not to be. We awoke that morning and opened the curtains to find a blizzard.

Downstairs, we opened the back door, and two feet of snow fell inside! It went on record as the worse snow fall we'd had in a long time.

Apparently, it was a very thin audience that night at The *City Varieties*. However, the BBC recording went ahead and we later watched the show on Television - which was wonderful - but, just a shame we couldn't have been there.

STEVE BARCLAY
Lincoln

What a joy and indeed a privilege to have the opportunity to add my memories of this theatrical gem, the Leeds *City Varieties* Theatre.

As a boy I would gaze at the TV screen watching the stars of *The Good Old Days* - Arthur Askey, Billy Dainty, Bernie Clifton and in particular Ken Dodd, my all time comedy hero.

I saw Tessie O'Shea make one of her 'full on' entrances (and exits) on that very stage and, being a 'banjo uke' player myself was mesmerised by her playing and of course, her professionalism with the audience.

Every week I would watch *The Good Old Days* and was totally star struck, watching people like Roy Hudd and Danny La Rue use the walk-way in their act.

Little did I realise then that in later life I would tread those same boards with Danny La Rue and offer my own tributes to Max Miller, Tessie O'Shea and George Formby.

One night after the show, I remember with great affection, being sat at the back of the stalls with Danny La Rue after we'd been in the bar to say 'Goodnight' to the audience (which Danny loved doing and insisted upon). Danny took my arm and said, "Come and sit with me luv while I tell you what this theatre means to me".

Danny told all about his many appearances there and all about Barney Colehan. He concluded by saying, "This theatre is Danny La Rue. This is where my heart belongs. So, young man enjoy your experience whilst you're working here with me at this sacred theatre." Then he took my hand, looked into my eyes and continued, "So, tomorrow at the matinee don't tell that awful joke about the parrot!"

THE SIMMONS BROTHERS

Kent

In 1982 my brother Keith and I were appearing in summer season at the *Spa Theatre* in Bridlington. Barney Colehan travelled over from Leeds to see the show and liked what we did. So, he immediately booked us for *The Good Old Days* to be recorded in the December.

We duly travelled up to the *City Varieties* to be met by Barney, who handed us an envelope. Upon reading the contents we discovered that owing to an industrial dispute the show that night wouldn't be recorded. As an audience was on its way he asked if we would still go ahead and do the show. We said, "Yes, of course we will," and along with the rest of the cast which included Ken Dodd and Anita Harris, it went ahead.

Thus began a very happy association with the *City Varieties*, Barney Colehan and Peter Sandeman that was to continue for the next 18 years and culminated in our appearing there over 70 times.

I remember Bernie Clifton handing his rather intricate lighting plot to Wally, the resident stage manager who was certainly not impressed with its content. Bernie's act that night consisted mostly of Bernie shouting, "Now Wally. Wally now. Now!" as he strived to get his lighting cue's right.

Perhaps our proudest moment was when we included in our act a song that was written and composed by our parents Mai and Clarry Simmons. The sheet music was published in the 1920's, sold for sixpence and was called, 'If at first you don't succeed chew peanuts'.

Another time Eartha Kitt threw a wobbly about the state and size of her dressing room. Barney went in to have a word with her. He returned saying, "She's fine now. I've told her Charlie Chaplin used that room." "Did he really? That's fantastic," said I. "Not really," said Barney, shrugging his shoulders, "I haven't a clue, but it's done the trick."

One of our tours with Norman Wisdom meant travelling to each theatre on a 49 seater coach. We gave George, the driver, a round of applause when he actually reversed down Swan Street to unload.

So many wonderful memories of a truly unique venue.

In the words of the great Max Miller, "They'll never be another one!"

STU FRANCIS
Bolton

As a young comic playing pubs and clubs around my home town of Bolton, I dreamed that one day I would play the *City Varieties*.

It was always my ambition to entertain there and, when I did, I was not disappointed. In fact I was in awe of this magnificent theatre which held so many memories of so many brilliant artistes.

I was thrilled to be in this special theatre I had heard so much about. Charlie Chaplin, Tessie O'Shea, Dora Bryan, Allan Randall, Max Miller - all names I greatly admired. To be on the same stage as those artistes was a tremendous privilege. I stood on stage taking my band-call and pictured them all standing in the same spot that I was standing in. Magical.

In the bar after every performance, where I go to say "hello" to the audience who have taken the time and trouble to leave their TV behind and come along to live theatre, I am fortunate to be surrounded by folk who still remember me for my many years in 'Crackerjack' (BBC) my appearances on 'The Comedians' and 'Seaside Special' (ITV) and even my part in the series 'Hey Brian' with Gemma Craven and Brian Marshall yet, the thing I pride the most, is being back where my heart wanted to be all those years ago - the *City Varieties*.

My only disappointment is that, as I leave the theatre, I look back and ask, "Why doesn't every town and city in the country have a *City Varieties*?"

There is nothing like live theatre and there is nothing like the *City Varieties*. I look forward to my return and saying "hello" once again to those wonderful warm audiences where we have a great time together.

I usually feel so powerful and strong after a performance at the City Varieties that I always have to say,

"Oooh. I could crush a grape!"

The Joseph Brothers had a solid fuel manually stoked boiler for the central heating. You had to keep a careful eye on it or the fire would go out and you'd be left with no heating in the auditorium.

So, there were many occasions when I'd be down in the cellar stoking the boiler in my dinner suit!

Peter Sandeman

Did you know that:-
In 1941 during a performance of the Pantomime, 'Babes In The Wood' a baby boy was born in the auditorium.

~

The ice-cream sold in the City Varieties was at one time made there.

~

The straw hats sold during performances of The Good Days are decorated personally (and lovingly) by the committee of The Friends of the theatre - so no two are exactly alike! (hats, not committee) -Ed

MARK SNEE
Leeds

Although I spent almost all my teenage years in Leeds before heading off to the Royal Academy of Music in London, it was not until several years after graduating that I first set foot in the *City Varieties*. By then I was working as Musical Director for well known artistes and touring the UK with various musical productions. It was good to at last see the Varieties on a tour list - it would be a cheap week for digs!

Peter Sandeman was the recently appointed general manager and Chris Fox, who I had worked with in a seaside variety show several years earlier, was house manager.

It's a great personal sadness that almost all the cast of that particular production have now passed on because despite few of them being widely known they were each enormously talented performers and extremely amusing, even if the *ad libs* invariably had more to do with off-stage shenanigans than with the plot. The only 'name' in the show that week was Bryan Johnson, the brother of Teddy Johnson (& Pearl Carr fame) who had been the UK entry in the 1960 Eurovision Song Contest, in which he came second with 'Looking High, High, High'. How I grew to hate that song......

Over the next three decades, I played the Varieties as Musical Director with many artistes. Live performance always carries a slight risk of the unexpected but there were rarely any serious mishaps. The only one I recall in Leeds was the performance when, half-way through the first half of the show, I was discreetly handed a note saying the 'top of the bill' was going on next (rather than closing the second half as usual). It soon became clear why; fortunately the notes were in tune even if the tempos fell victim to the gin - an occupational hazard for performers, it seems. It was a sad end for this wonderful lady who had spent a lifetime on stage and had many hit records.

In 1993, I arranged for Russ Conway to come up to Leeds to judge the Leeds Pub Piano Playing Competition (which ran alongside the

Mark Snee with The Beverley Sisters, for whom he was Musical Director from 1984 until they retired from performing some twenty years later.

International Pianoforte Competition as a sort of drinking man's alternative). Russ was a great personal friend, who I worked with as Musical Director for fifteen years until shortly before he died in November 2000. As a result of his visit, Peter Sandeman booked him for the following season of *The Good Old Days*, although it almost ended in tears when, a week before he was due to appear, Russ discovered there was no smoking allowed in the dressing rooms.

My happiest memories of the Varieties come from the Leeds heats and Yorkshire final of the national 'Silver Stars' competition, which I played for over several years. There were some excellent contestants as well as a few who were 'musically challenged'. Most were nervous but it was their big day and for several the realisation of a long-held ambition to perform on the stage of the Varieties, so I always did my best to help and encourage them. (Although sight-reading 'Nessun Dorma' in 'five flats' one minute and busking some rock and roll offering in an uncertain key the next was almost as challenging as anything I have ever done professionally - even the concert pianist John Briggs was impressed when he was a judge one year.) My good friend Ronnie Bottomley played percussion and we always enjoyed a bit of banter with judges John Thorpe, Joan Elder and others after the shows. BBC's *Look North* and YTV's *Calendar* took turns to cover the finals.

The *City Varieties* was a very special place during these years, despite its delapidated interior prior to refurbishment. I'm sure that's because it's people who make a venue successful, warm and inviting, and Peter and his team achieved that *par excellence* year in, year out for more than a quarter of a century. I'm priviledged to have been part of it.

KEITH LOUDON
Adel, Leeds

One of my charitable objectives as Lord Mayor was to enhance the experience of the senior generation and I spent many happy hours organising and providing entertainment, events, parties and lunches for anyone in Leeds who wanted to come.

It was a logistical nightmare in some respects - how to get folk from A to B - but my team rallied round and got folk to every event. Some folk came to everything and eventually I knew all their names, where they lived and what they liked to watch on TV. It felt as if I was meeting up with old friends.

Whilst everyone thoroughly enjoyed all the events telling me how wonderful it was to get out of the house for a change and to meet like-minded folk in a safe environment, I still wanted to do more - something different for them. I wanted to give them a proper show in a proper theatre. A show to remember. But, not just in any theatre. I wanted this to be special, something truly unforgettable. So I chose our own Leeds theatre the *City Varieties*.

I had always loved the *City Varieties* and decided to put on a special performance aimed specifically at people from the older generation and, with the enthusiastic support from the General Manager, Peter Sandeman we got the show on the road.

Johnny Dennis agreed to fulfill the vital role of Chairman and did a brilliant job. We invited our local songbird Caroline Fields and rapid-fire comedian Peter (machine gun) Wallis. Both were a tremendous success and, to tell the truth, I still sing some of Caroline's songs (when no-one's listening) and tell some of Peter's jokes in my speeches! We also had artistes from further afield too. It was a great variety bill.

The atmosphere was second to none as it always is in that theatre. It was a great evening with dancers, laughter, music and song and even though no-one paid to get in, the late arrivals (who were asked to sit on the side benches until the interval) were heard to comment, 'How come we're sitting here?'

As the saying goes, "You can't please all of the people all of the time!" But, I tried!

Former Lord Mayor Of Leeds - 1993/1994
The City Varieties is very dear to my heart.

104

RUBY SWANN
Otley - Aged 94

My first memory of the *City Varieties* is going on the tram into Leeds from Brudenell Road, where we lived at the time. It was a huge thrill as it was my first ride on this heavy, noisy, rattling mode of transport (we usually took the bus). In Leeds we went to The Kardoma Café for afternoon tea before making our way up to the theatre for the pantomime.

It seemed to me that there were hundreds, if not thousands of people, all milling around outside waiting for the doors to open. Everyone was excited especially the children, who were jumping up and down and asking when they would be allowed inside.

Everyone wore hats and coats and I remember I wore I an emerald green coat, hat and matching muff which had been bought from Hitchins Store in Briggate, Leeds. (I think that, much later it became Woolworths). They were my best clothes. The coat was a little big but, as mum said, I would 'grow into it'. I had short white socks and black patent leather shoes and felt very smart. In the pocket of my coat was a clean white handkerchief and a threepenny bit which my Grandma had given me.

When the doors opened everyone formed an orderly queue to get inside. It was amazing - all 'plush' inside with boxes, balconies, railings and many ornate features. Then the lights went down, the pantomime began and I was enthralled. When the dancers came on stage I decided there and then I wanted to be a dancer. When the singers came on I decided I might like to be a singer instead. When I grew up I did both! I loved the *City Varieties* then and I love it now. Happy Anniversaries.

BOBBIE CAPLIN OBE
Alwoodley, Leeds

Going back a very long time - sixty-four years to be exact I remember skipping school early one afternoon, as we did whenever the opportunity presented itself to see the famous Phyllis Dixey, who was billed as

The Girl The Lord Chamberlain Banned.

With my other school friends, we arrived at the *City Varieties* early in order to ensure front row seats. Whilst we enjoyed the rest of the show, it was Phyllis Dixey we had come to see.

When she appeared, the audience erupted with hearty appreciation. The applause was, at first, deafening. Then, a gradual hush descended over the auditorium in anticipation of what was to come. You could hear a pin drop. Slowly, with bated breath and hoping no-one could see us, we carefully took our pea-shooters from our pockets. We also hoped that, with good aim, we could get her to move! On occasions we were successful!

Great Memories of Dear Friends
Stanley Joseph
Barney Colehan
and
Cecil Korer

JIM HORSLEY
Ilkley, Yorkshire

For as long as I can remember, I have been fascinated by 'live' theatre and especially Variety. My earliest memories of the *City Varieties* are from the early 1950's when I used to go with friends to see the nude shows. They played most weeks featuring artistes such as Phyllis Dixey, Peaches Page and Jane of The Daily Mirror. We used to sit on the benches, which ran alongside the sides of the balcony (I think the seats were 9d). From there you could often see the artistes in the wings, waiting to go on stage. We thought the shows were very daring (to 16 year old boys). Although the 'nudes' were not allowed to move they often formed a tableaux depicting a scene from history. It would amuse us when the curtains were drawn aside by stage hands with dirty shoes showing under the curtains.

My favourite stripper was Rhoda Rogers who had a very beautiful backside! I did not see her again until the 1970's when I was invited to the Water Rats Ball in London and was introduced to her as she was then the wife of the 'King Rat', Cyril and very elegantly dressed.

In the 1960's I was responsible for putting on regular Old Time Music Hall Shows at The Kings Hall, Ilkley and, one year we decided to engage 'The Black and White Minstrels' to appear for three successive nights at Ilkley, the Royal Hall in Harrogate and at Leeds *City Varieties*. We had full houses at all three venues and raised a substantial sum for the 'Save The Children' fund and the Disabled.

It was a great relief when, in 1987 Leeds City Council bought the *City Varieties* from the Joseph Brothers and ensured its future as Britain's Oldest Working Music Hall. The recent refurbishment under the direction of Peter Sandeman is quite superb and a lasting tribute to those who treasure this little gem of a theatre.

Part of the enjoyment of going to the *City Varieties* has been in meeting many of the artistes in the Circle Bar. However, I remember many years ago taking our children to see 'Babes in The Wood' and to my surprise the Babes - who turned out to be two middle aged ladies in their fifties - were in the bar at the interval having cigarettes and gin and tonic!

Jim is Past Chairman of the Friends of the Kings Hall and Winter Garden, Ilkley

Photograph by kind permission of Barry Wilkinson

JOHN BOUCHIER
Cambridgeshire

I have been fortunate enough to play the *City Varieties* in Leeds ten times. The first bill I can find is dated 11th February, 1963, but I remember playing it prior to that with the famous strip artiste Blondie Haigh.

In the late 40's I started my career at the age of 14 (and a half!) at Collins Music Hall in London, which was similar in many ways to the *City Varieties* as a venue. This meant that when I played Leeds I felt very much at home. Barney Colehan used my act twice during the TV days of *The Good Old Days*, both with Ken Dodd topping the bill. This was delightful for me as I had worked with Ken many times before and had appeared for a season with him at *The London Palladium*.

As *The Good Old Days* was an outside broadcast, after every act had performed, the recording was stopped and the tape checked to make sure everything had worked; a nightmare for patter acts like me and Ken as, if it was not perfect you had to repeat the act to an audience who had already heard all the gags five minutes before!

It is not so easy to get a laugh the second time around so it was always a relief to get the 'all clear' from the outside broadcast team in the van parked just outside the theatre.

I think the *City Varieties* is the only theatre I ever remember playing with a blank wall as you exit stage right. If you went there by mistake you were stuck there trying your hardest not to be seen until the tabs came down at the interval or at the end of the show. Most acts did it once and got stuck there but I imagine they didn't repeat it! (I know I didn't do it again!)

The audiences made up of regular and loyal visitors to the *City Varieties* must have seen this happen on several occasions and timed how long the act would have to stand there for!

Since the current Music Hall seasons started, I have been on a further six bills and, have loved every minute of the town, the audiences and this iconic gem of a theatre.

I send my sincere good wishes to the Friends of this unique and beautiful venue.

DON MACLEAN MBE

Solihull, West Midlands

I did my very first Summer Season 'Follies on Parade' in Skegness in 1964. The first job I managed to get after that was a week at the *City Varieties*. I'd seen this wonderful theatre featured on BBC television in *The Good Old Days* produced by the marvellous Barney Colehan.

I was to appear on the *The Good Old Days* several times during the years ahead but for now the good people of Leeds were to be given a whole week in which to assess my talent. I arrived in the city full of expectations and scanned the shop windows for posters advertising this week's variety - keen to see my name on the bill.

When I did eventually see a poster it stopped me in my tracks. My name was there alright, in very small letters. The title of the show dominated, 'Prison Without Bras'. Apart from me and one of the funniest double acts ever to step on a stage, Gordon and Bunny Jay, the bill comprised three strippers and a nude Chinese fire-eater. She wasn't easy for a lad from a good Catholic home to cope with. I've forgotten her name but not her aroma; even to this day I can't smell Ronson Lighter Fuel without getting slightly excited.

On Monday night I died the death of a dog - no-one laughed, not a single titter, I was distraught. Stanley Joseph came backstage afterwards. I was convinced he'd come to pay me off, "You're not funny son, don't bother to come in tomorra!" But no, he ignored me in my misery. He was there to take issue with one of the strippers who came on dressed as a Red Indian with interesting war paint and proceeded to do strange things with a tomahawk.

"You leave that bloody thing in the dressing room tomorra night, I'll get closed down else," threatened Stanley.

Gordon and Bunny kept me sane. They were doing three spots while I was mercifully only doing two. "All comics die here," explained Gordon. "They've just come to see the flesh. If you thought tonight was bad wait for tomorrow's matinee." He was right. A couple of dozen men were scattered round the stalls. As I came on nearly every one of them opened up a newspaper and read it until I'd left the stage to the sound of my own feet. This was a far cry from the tweeness of 'Follies on Parade'.

What a week. I stayed in pro digs called Novello House run by a permanently cravatted chap who kept telling me that, in a certain light, my profile resembled 'Dear Ivor' - the Novello after whom the house had been named. I had only one good night in the theatre and that was Thursday when the place was packed with students from Leeds University. They'd come to heckle and they were good at it. They heckled the strippers - "Keep em on!" They heckled the nude Chinese fire-eater, "There's a different slant on things!" but mostly they heckled the comics.

I gave as good as I got and was rewarded with cheers and applause which enabled me to survive Friday and Saturday. I was so pleased to leave that place.

That week was an experience I had no wish to repeat and yet, several years later, the *City Varieties* was to play it's part in a surprising career change for me.

By 1990 things had changed at the theatre, no more disrobing ladies, just variety with an Old Time Music Hall feel and a different top of the bill every week. I was booked as one of those. On the Friday evening I received a phone call from Yorkshire Television. Was it true that I was a practicing Catholic? I confirmed that I was. In that case they'd like me to go along to the studio, after I'd finished on stage that evening, to take part in a live discussion about religion.

I arrived and was introduced to the other participants - a Yorkshireman who had converted to Islam and a Methodist Minister, Frank Topping. The presenter was a warm, friendly chap called James Whale. Friendly that is until the programme started. The red light went on, the floor manager signaled

James who looked into the camera and said, "Most of you out there are saying to yourselves 'religion, that's a load of b*****ks'." Three jaws dropped as one. I hadn't expected anything like that. James then started on poor Frank who was still gob-smacked by the opening gambit and managed little by way of response. James, with blood-lust dripping from every pore, moved to his next victim, "And you Muslims," he accused, "You're not interested in religion, all you want to do is get your hands round the throat of Salman Rushdie." The poor chap was as non-plussed as Frank. I was thankful that I'd had a few seconds to gather my thoughts.

When James rounded on me I was ready, "You Roman Catholics are all obsessed with birth control. Do you and your wife practice birth control?" I quickly remembered every condom joke I'd ever heard and selected one at random.

Everything he threw at me I fielded with a gag. He could think quick but I could think quicker. Asked by a caller if he believed in God, James Whale said, "Well, yes I suppose I do, there that's ruined my credibility." I decided to take him on. "Ruined your credibility? That's the first thing you've said tonight that's had any credibility." I was taking over but he didn't seem to mind.

I explained how being a believer and publicly identifying myself as a Christian was something of which I was proud. I'd never had such an opportunity to stand up for my church before and I was relishing it. The programme finished and James discarded his television persona as though it were an old suit and reverted to the charming man I'd first met. The controller of BBC Radio 2 and the head of BBC Religious Broadcasting just happened to be watching that show. The following week they asked me to present, *Good Morning Sunday*. BBC Radio's flagship religious programme, which I did for 15 years until 2006. What a career change! What a 'lucky break!' And all due to the fabulous *City Varieties*.

The Queens
Leeds

Special events
at a stunning,
landmark venue

The Art Deco charm, elegant banqueting suites and superb service will ensure that your special event is one to be remembered by all.

From elaborate charity balls and award ceremonies, to intimate private dining; we provide both the dramatic backdrop and the exceptional level of service required to guarantee the success of each and every event.

Please ask us about our Christmas and New Year's Eve parties

- Prime location in the heart of Leeds
- Delicious menus tailored to your needs
- The capacity to hold up to 500 guests
- Fantastic packages available for your convenience including our Charity and Special Event Package
- 18 beautiful QClub Suites plus Executive Lounge on our exclusive top floor
- Valet car parking available at an additional cost

The Queens sends good wishes to The Friends of The City Varieties for the future

0113 2431323
queensevents@QHotels.co.uk
www.QHotels.co.uk/thequeens

Green Tourism
SILVER

PAUL DANIELS
Wargrave, Wokingham

"You'll like this...Not a lot...But you'll like it". Like millions of others I watched *The Good Old Days* on television. I would frequently scream at the director who would cut away from the act to show the reaction of the audience. We had no idea what they were reacting to because we couldn't see the highlight of the act.

Years went by before I could get to perform on the tiny sloping stage which, from watching television I expected to be much bigger.

Backstage was even smaller. Those conditions could not detract from the astonishing and wonderful sense of REAL theatre when you walk out in front of the audience. This is one of my favourite places in which to perform. Add the sense of show-business history to the ambiance and design of the auditorium and your skins starts to tingle as you walk on. Long may it reign.

RUNNING ORDER - "THE GOOD OLD DAYS" (No. 155).

TELERECORDING: 4th NOVEMBER, 1973.

OPENING ROUTINE & CHAIRMAN'S INTRODUCTION

PLAYERS THEATRE COMPANY 'ASCOT' SCENA
                    15 - 11. ENGLISH GARDEN   F/S.

LOS GAUCHOS   17 - 2.   BRIGHTON PAVILION F/S

GEORGIA BROWN   14 - 12. REGENT STREET   ¾/S.

RAY ALAN   10 - 25. MAXIM'S   ¾/S.

MICHEL GALLOIS   16 - 34. CORRIDOR   ¾/S.

TERRY SCOTT   11 - 10. MARKET SQUARE   ¾/S.

GEORGIA BROWN & PLAYERS THEATRE COMPANY
                    18 - 7.   PICCADILLY   F/S.

FINALE & CLOSING ROLLER CAPTION

(Above) A Fly Sheet from Tim Quinn dated 4th Nov 1973. TV recording Of The Good Old Days showing the Running Order, Cloths and Lighting for each artiste

TIM QUINN
Leeds

Back in 1969 aged 16, I clambered over the bins, boxes and general garbage that littered the narrow alleyway to the World Famous *City Varieties* stage-door in search of work. What a stroke of luck. The perfect time and place. I stayed there as backstage crew for the next very happy eight years. During that time each year comprised two runs of music hall shows with the world's longest running panto smack bang wallop in between and the BBC would record a season of their *Good Old Days* each year. This allowed me to meet such legends as Arthur Askey, Mr. Pastry, Ted Ray, Danny La Rue, Ken Dodd, Roy Castle, Albert Modley, Charlie Drake, and Bruce Forsyth. Fantastic performances whether viewed from the Flys or the Limes.

But, the real entertainment came with the extraordinary characters I was to meet backstage. The Joseph brothers, who would have made a good double act themselves. Wally Coe, the Stage Manager, a real Dickensian creation. Fag permanently in mouth, ash down his front, dog at his feet, and a 'Gorgeous Gaiety Girl' on his knee.

I remember on several occasions when the rest of the stage crew failed to turn up for a matinee that Wally and I would run the whole show. I must have done the two-minute mile between Flys, stage and the Limes on those days. And oh, those Gorgeous Gaiety Girls. Most of them were plucked from obscurity behind Woolworths counters and most of them ended up back behind Woolworths counters. But what a glorious memory to have been a 'Gorgeous Gaiety Girl' treading the boards at the *City Varieties*.

I fell in love whilst at the ' Verts' - not with a GGG but with a Robinson Crusoe in 1975. He was played by Pippa Boulter, daughter of John Boulter, a lead singer with the *Black & White Minstrels*. She didn't know whether her dad was black or white until she was about four!

During ' Jack and The Beanstalk' I remember knocking the giant with an early incoming cloth from the Flys. Toppled from his stilts, he fell with a crash onto the xylophone which the audience loved. Someone shouted from stalls, "Keep it in!" Then there was Eartha Kitt...who looked into my eyes and has stayed there for 40 years! That is star quality.

Wally Coe on the left, with a young Keith Harris and Orvill. Wally was the Stage Manager at the City Varieties for many years.
Photo Courtesy of Tim Quinn

Tim Quinn
backstage at the City Varieties

DON REID
Winsford, Cheshire

My treasured memory of the *City Varieties* concerns two of the comedy greats, Norman Collier and Neville King. They invented anarchy!

Neville and I were supporting Joan Regan during the Music Hall season and I was first and second half opening comic. Neville was first half closer, second top of the bill. Our dressing rooms were at the top and level with the circle.

Neville was walking into his dressing room, carrying his Grand-dad doll and I asked, "How did it go?" "Fine!" came the reply, "Until I got him out" - obviously meaning the doll.

Back came another voice which I knew was the dolls, "Take no notice of him, I didn't do anything!" There followed an argument between the two of them - (Neville and the doll) getting more heated with a few swear words creeping in.

I thought 'sod this,' left them to it and went to make a cuppa in the green room. I still don't know if it was real or for my benefit. He was a genius as was Norman Collier.

Between houses on the Saturday we went for meal with the whole company, across at Nash's fish restaurant. Norman had come to see Neville socially and joined us. Picture the scene. We are all sat chatting and reading the menus, some still in 'slap', when suddenly Neville and Norman have an invisible dog fight under the table and keep asking each other, "Can't you control him?" "It's your dog, not mine!" "Why did you have to bring him? You knew mine was coming." "You know they don't get on!" The dogs barked and woofed. Snarled and fought.

The other diners didn't know what to think and kept looking under our table but, even though there was the sound of dogs there was nothing to be seen. Even the staff began to look across. The dogs fought courageously until the food arrived and were then told to ' lie still' and we all just sat there as if it was perfectly normal.

There's no business et cetera.

ROY HUDD OBE

Croydon, Surrey

Two great Friends of this beautiful little theatre were Clarice and Joyce. Clarice is still with us but alas, Joyce is not. The two of them, Gert and Daisy as I called them, were always backstage when Music Hall dates were on. They were great company. They'd make us cups of tea, dress us, repair costumes, make us laugh and do anything that made life easier for all of us in the show. Best of all they boosted our egos and encouraged us. The audience got a better performance after the girls had given us a pep talk.

One evening just before I was going on, I stooped to pick up a prop I'd dropped. A ripping sound came from my nether regions - NO! It wasn't! My trousers had split from waistband to crutch. "Too many noshes at Nash's", I thought. I cried for help and the girls appeared with needle and cotton.

Someone quickly alerted Johnny (Dennis) to the problem and as he ad-libbed my introduction (that truly made Leonard Sachs wordy announcements sound like one-liners) the girls were chasing me round backstage sewing the trousers together as I desperately gathered my props. I got on-stage only to be immediately hauled back into the wings by Clarice and she and Joyce sewed the final two or three stitches. I covered my return by trying to explain the girls were two of my groupies who followed me everywhere.

Clarice and Joyce were the heart and soul of the *City Varieties* Music Hall weeks and that night they did a deed far beyond the call of duty. Now, whenever I work at the *City Varieties* I always take two pairs of trousers - with quick release braces.

Roy has been a Member of The Grand Order of Water Rats for 40 years and was King Rat for their 100th Anniversary and for the Millennium.

To date he has had 55 years in Showbusiness. Roy, Debbie, Bella and Joan send their love. (Bella is a Llasa apso and Joan is a Schnauzer) - Ed

Peter with Clive Dunn and Johnny Dennis

Peter with Clarice and Joyce

Barney and Peter

The Circle Bar

Gordon Kaye, Tony Adams, Beryl Kemp and Les Shavers

Stanley and Michael Joseph, taken outside
the Headrow entrance to the City Varieties.
Photo courtesy of The Showman's Guild
at rossparry.co.uk

May every visit to our

venues be enjoyable

and memorable

Leeds Grand Theatre & Opera House
46 New Briggate
Leeds
LS1 6NZ
www.leedsgrandtheatre.com
Box Office: 0870 122 2820

Hyde Park Picture House
73 Brudenell Road
Headingley
Leeds
LS6 1JD
www.hydeparkpicturehouse.co.uk
Tele: 0113 275 2045

DAME VERA LYNN OBE
East Sussex

Dame Vera sends her good wishes to "The Friends of the City Varieties Music Hall"
Dame Vera Lynn D.B.E, LLD, M. Mus

Amongst the artistes booked by Barney Colehan
for the televised productions of

'The Good Old Days'

were

Jack Douglas
Mary O'Hara
Allan Randall
Bernard Cribbins
Arthur Askey
Bernie Clifton
Roy Hudd
June Bronhill
Charlie Chester
Dora Bryan
Moria Anderson
Les Dawson
Ken Dodd
Barry Cryer
Roy Castle
Keith Harris
Pat Mooney
Kenneth McKellar
John Inman
Billy Dainty
Rod Hull
Patrick Fyffe and
George Logan
(Hinge and Bracket),
Ron Moody
Larry Grayson
Vince Hill
Max Bygraves
Millicent Martin

Rita Morris
Jessie Matthews
Julia McKenzie
Fenella Fielding
Frankie Vaughan
The Beverley Sisters
Jan Hunt
Mike Reid
Ted and Hilda Durante
Clive Dunn
Danny La Rue
Frank Carson
Edward Woodward
Hylda Baker
Eartha Kitt
Richard Herne
Ronnie Corbett
Rosemary Squires
Peggy Mount
Ken Goodwin
Tessie O'Shea
Lorna Dallas
Val Doonican
Sandie Shaw
Bruce Forsyth
Jill Summers
Stubby Kaye
Jimmy Tarbuck
Eddie Large and Syd Little

Barbara Windsor
Don Maclean
Joseph Locke
The Clark Brothers
Jack Platts
Clinton Ford
Albert Modley
Ted Ray
George Chisholm
Frankie Holmes
Beryl Reid
Sandy Powell
Don Smoothey
Reg Varney
Joan Turner
The Gaunt Brothers
Kim Cordell
Gracie Fields
Jimmy and Brian
(The Patton Brothers)
Freddie Frinton
Colin Crompton
Tod Slaughter
Eric Morecambe
and Ernie Wise
Cardew Robinson
Charlie Williams
Neville King
Norman Collier

and
Our very own Leeds lad, comedian Peter (machine gun) Wallis
(televised on the 8th February, 1974)

Bernard Herrman was the Musical Director
and Doreen Hermitage was the Choreographer